details détails details

elements in architecture
details details details

EDITED BY OSCAR RIERA OJEDA
TEXT BY MARK PASNIK
PHOTOGRAPHY BY PAUL WARCHOL

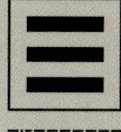

EVERGREEN

design by oscar riera ojeda and lucas guerra
layout by oscar riera ojeda

© 2008 EVERGREEN GmbH, Köln

Original edition:
© 2003 by Rockport Publishers, Inc.
Original title:
Architecture in detail. Elements

German translation:
Nora von Mühlendahl, Ludwigsburg
French translation:
Anne-Catherine Reynolds, Schaffhausen
Dutch translation:
Marianne Palm for Deul & Spanjaard, Groningen

ISBN 978-3-8365-0342-6
Printed in China

To the memory of GM, who ceaselessly
shared her love of words and buildings.
— MP

In remembrance of Teresa Testone
Pellegrino, whose spirit remains vivid.
En memoria de Teresa Testone Pellegrino,
cuyo espíritu permanece vivo.
— ORO

inhalt sommaire inhoud

einleitung introduction inleiding **7**
türen portes deuren **14**
fenster fenêtres ramen **28**
wände murs muren **44**
säulen colonnes zuilen **62**
oberlichter lucarnes dakramen **82**
vordächer auvents overkappingen **98**
treppen escaliers trappen **110**
geländer rampes leuningen **132**
trennwände écrans schermen **160**
einbauten placards kasten **180**
danksagung remerciements dankbetuiging **192**

Hybride Formen

In einem zur Ikone gewordenen Bauwerk der Architektur des 20. Jahrhunderts verbreitert sich das Treppengeländer am oberen Ende zu einem Sitz. Dessen Form entspricht der des Handlaufs, verändert sich jedoch zu einem durchgehenden Profil, das sich der menschlichen Form anpasst, ohne zwischen der Rückenlehne der Bank und dem Geländer zu unterscheiden (Abb. 1), einfach als unteilbare Erweiterung, die über ihre Dualität hinwegtäuscht. ■ Eine solche zwingende Dualität ergab sich, als wir dieses Buch erarbeiteten. Die Reihe sollte ursprünglich zu einer Sammlung von Architekturelementen werden, funktional klarer und ablesbarer Bestandteile eines Gebäudes. Das Buch sollte ein Katalog heutzutage üblicher, kleinmaßstäblicher Details werden, ein allgemein gültiges Verzeichnis typischer Bauteile, das die Vielfalt der gegenwärtigen Baupraxis wiedergibt. ■ Beim Durchforsten von Paul Warchols Archiv mit Fotos aus drei Jahrzehnten erkannten wir jedoch bald, dass viele Details sich nicht in bestimmte Kategorien einordnen lassen. Heutzutage sind Details nicht mehr unbedingt eindeutig, unveränderbar oder gar identifizierbar. So attraktiv die Vorstellung auch sein mochte, es wurde uns klar, dass die heutige Architektur sich besser durch Hervorhebung von Details dokumentieren ließ, die in keinen Katalog passen. Wir konnten die Geschichte nicht ignorieren. ■ Die eigentliche Vorstellung vom Detail als eindeutigem Bauteil entwickelte sich aus den Publikationen über Architektur. Die einflussreichsten von ihnen, die Bücher Vitruvs und Palladios, sind Kataloge von Bauelementen, die ein zentrales Verzeichnis des klassischen Vokabulars bilden. Vitruv klassifizierte die Archetypen des Tempels und beschrieb drei

zugt vorgeschriebene und bindende Richtlinien. Ein noch weiter verbreitetes Phänomen ist die Abhängigkeit der Bauindustrie von nur wenigen spezifischen Vorgaben, die zu einer rigorosen Standardisierung von Details führt. ■ Im Extremfall entsteht das ganze Bauwerk nur durch Verbindung dieser festgelegten Elemente in neuer Form. Dadurch wird das kreative Potenzial begrenzt, Überlegungen über die eigentlichen Aufgaben der Elemente werden verhindert. ■ Wir hoffen, dass dieses Buch zu einem provokativen Auslöser kreativen Nachdenkens über Bauelemente wird. Wenn Klassizismus die Suche nach „festen und unwandelbaren Gesetzen"[3] bedeutet, so folgen wir im gegenwärtigen Bauen einer anderen Strategie, die sich mit Konflikten, Widersprüchen und Spannungen in der Architektur auseinandersetzt. ■ Im Verlauf der Entwicklung der Moderne blieben die Elemente gestalterischer Mittelpunkt des „neuen Zeitalters" und seiner Suche nach neuen Formen. Neue Vorstellungen innerhalb der Moderne veränderten jedoch die Definition der Elemente; neue Auffassungen vom Raum zeigten sich in Braques oder Picassos kubistischen Gemälden, in denen Objekte aus mehreren Blickwinkeln zugleich dargestellt wurden. Das ermöglichte den Architekten, die Funktionsweise von Elementen zu verändern: Eine Glasscheibe verdoppelte sich zur Tür, ein Dach wurde auch zu einem Garten. ■ Die auferstandene Moderne hat eine außergewöhnliche Wende von verbundenen Details zu Zwittern durchgemacht; sie vereint zwar wieder verschiedene Elemente, verzichtet aber auf die Identität der Bauteile zugunsten der Untrennbarkeit des größeren Ganzen. Spannungen verbleiben in den Beziehungen der Elemente zueinander, die jetzt nahtlos und viel komplexer als die Grund-

einleitung introduction inleiding

MARK PASNIK

Ordnungen, die er als „Grundbegriffe" betrachtete und die nach üblichem Gebrauch so angewendet werden sollten: „Denn kein Tempel kann ohne Symmetrie und Proportion eine vernünftige Formgebung haben, wenn seine Glieder nicht in einem bestimmten Verhältnis zueinander stehen."[1] Er betonte die festgelegte und vorbestimmte Kodifizierung aller Elemente der klassischen Architektur. ■ Palladio begann mit der Beschreibung der Komponenten, aus denen ein Gebäude besteht, vom Fundament über Wände, Säulen, Räume, Böden, Decken, Kamin, Treppen (Abb. 10) bis zum Dach. Darauf beschrieb er den Ablauf, nach dem ein Gebäude errichtet wird, und er betonte anschließend die Beziehung aller Elemente zum größeren Bauwerk, bei dem „jedem Teil der ihm angemessene Ort und die Lage zugeteilt werden".[2] Die Betonung liegt wieder auf der „Entsprechung" der Teile mit den Konventionen. ■ Diese Tradition hat lange Bestand gehabt. Noch heute erkennen wir eine klassische Aufteilung in zwei unterschiedliche ideologische Lager. Das eine behandelt Elemente als wiederholbare Formen, von denen identische Details von einem Projekt zum nächsten übertragen werden können. Das andere bevor-

formen der Klassik miteinander verflochten sind in einer an Maurits Escher erinnernden Vortäuschung von Überschneidungen, Widersprüchen und Schichtungen. Die eigentliche Bestimmung der Elemente hat sich gelockert; den Architekten bietet sich dadurch ein Potenzial, neue Formen zu erschaffen und den Menschen neue Nutzungsarten des Raumes anzubieten. ■ In zwei neueren, mit dem Computer erstellten Avantgarde-Entwürfen wird der Kern des Gebäudes betont. In einem Modell von Elizabeth Diller und Ricardo Scofidio – Architekten, die für die Verbindung der Medien bekannt sind – besteht das ganze Bauwerk aus einem durchgehenden, in zweifacher Richtung gebogenen Band, das sich in eine ungebrochene, gewellte Oberfläche auflöst, die zwischen ihren beiden Ebenen das Tragsystem enthält (Abb. 3–4). Der Kern lässt Räume entstehen, die Studenten und Lehrer zur Kommunikation mit den Betrachtern anregen. Die Architekten unterstreichen die Fähigkeit eines Details, soziale Aktivitäten auszulösen. ■ In kleinerem Maßstab zeigt das Torus House von Preston Scott Cohen einen ebenso komplexen Kern (Abb. 5), der konventionell im Zentrum des Hauses liegt, die Wohnräume abtrennt und den Carport mit der Dachterrasse verbindet, jedoch mit undefinierten Funktionen: Ist das ein Treppenhaus, ein Innenhof, ein Lichtschacht oder alles zugleich? Dadurch wird unsere erste Deutung des Kerns erheblich komplexer: Das noch als solches identifizierbare Objekt geht an seinen Rändern in Decke und Boden über und wird zum Bestandteil der es umgebenden Fläche. Die vielen Erscheinungsformen des Kerns sind „untrennbar vom Ganzen geworden".[4] ■ Architekten brechen mit den überholten Konventionen und äußern Zweifel an den eindeutigen Formen der Elemente. Ihnen bieten sich neue Wege des Denkens, für Experimente, Auseinandersetzungen oder Überraschungen, die den restriktiven Definitionen der Formtypen widersprechen. ■ Wir möchten noch eine weiteren Punkt erwähnen: Da Elemente den sie umgebenden Bau gestalten, wird unsere Wahrnehmung derselben von äußeren Faktoren bestimmt. Elemente kommunizieren häufig über einen Raum hinweg, bilden gestalterische Momente, die zusammen eine komplettere Aussage machen. Obgleich dieser Prozess auch in der Klassik und in Scarpas Werk zu beobachten ist, hat die gegenwärtige Diskussion den Einfluss der äußeren Faktoren auf unsere Wahrnehmung von Elementen erweitert. Gordon Matta-Clarks „Four Corners" setzen allgemein bekannte Teile von Dach und Wänden in einen neuen Kontext (Abb. 6) und werfen die Frage auf, ob das Element selbst oder sein Kontext von Bedeutung ist. Sind Donald Judds Arbeiten in Marfa als Einzelstücke ohne den Rest der Sammlung oder das sie umgebende Gelände zu verstehen (Abb.7–8)? Kontextuelle Faktoren sind nicht nur räumlicher, sondern unter anderem auch materieller, ethischer, sozialer Natur. Zur Fähigkeit eines

tige Wirkung der Details, die unser Erlebnis jedes baulichen Umfelds bereichert. ■ Wie viele der in diesem Buch gezeigten Details sind solche Elemente nur kleine Teile eines Gebäudes, sie haben aber große gestalterische Bedeutung und sind von herausragender Schönheit, Poesie, Provokation, Widerspruch, Aussage oder Spannung erfüllt. Sie bereichern uns in den seltenen Momenten, da wir Kunst in Komponenten der Alltagsarchitektur entdecken. ■ Es sind Zeichen der Handschrift des Architekten, sie bilden die Grundlage eines persönlichen Dialogs zwischen dem Planer und dem Betrachter und sind dazu bestimmt, unsere Sinne anzusprechen. ■ Zum Beispiel sind die Gemälde von Mimi Moncier Auflistungen der verschiedenen Dinge aus ihrer unmittelbaren Umgebung (Abb. 9). Sie zeigt auf ihren Bildern ringförmige Figuren in intensiven Farben, die als „fokussierende Elemente agieren" und dazu auffordern, „den Blick auf Farben als Wunschobjekte"[5] zu richten. ■ Wir haben den Band als Katalog von Gattungen aufgezogen, der vielleicht eher die aktuellen und pluralistischen Merkmale eines Sammelwerks aufweist als von absoluter Konsequenz geprägt ist. Wir haben die Projekte in Kategorien aufgeteilt, die wir zum Maßstab für Innovation, Kreativität und Komplexität der hier vorgestellten Details nehmen. Wo sie von diesem System abweichen, ihre Einmaligkeit ausdrücken und sich der Klassifizierung widersetzen, ist das entscheidende Moment, welches unsere Bewunderung verdient.

Anmerkungen

1 Vitruv, *Zehn Bücher über Architektur* (ab 33. v. Chr., Wissenschaftliche Buchgesellschaft, Darmstadt 1991), S. 137. ■ 2 Andrea Palladio, *Die vier Bücher zur Architektur* (1570, Verlag für Architektur Artemis,

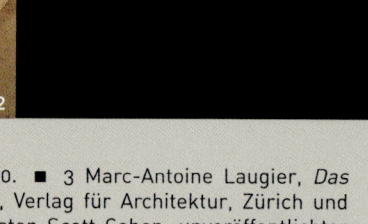

Details, Ideen auszudrücken, tragen Lichtreflexion, Verhalten und Produktionsmethode bei. Die künstlerische Wirkung eines Details liegt sowohl außerhalb von als auch in ihm. ■ All das zeigt sich an den Projekten auf den folgenden Buchseiten, welche die Definition von Details in Frage stellen. Ein Oberlicht erweitert sich zu einem Wasserbecken (Abb.11, S. 94–97), eine Metallstütze verbindet sich mit einer hölzernen Bank (S. 74–75), deren Rückenlehne sowohl den Sitzenden schützt als auch die statische Last des vom Haus auskragenden Volumens ausdrückt. Ein Regalsystem entsteht aus ausgefahrenen Schubladen, die wieder eingeschoben werden und eine geschlossene Holzwand bilden können (S. 182–183) – das Detail verändert sich ständig. Hölzerne Kleiderschränke werden ihrer Bezüge beraubt und durch Abstraktion (S. 4–5) wiederhergestellt, so dass sie nicht wie Verkaufsvitrinen, sondern eher wie Werke von Donald Judd aussehen. Eine Kapelle hat zwei Türen, die untrennbare, mit der Fassade zusammenhängende Bestandteile sind (S. 20–23); ovale Fenster bilden ein Muster, das nicht mit den Türen, sondern mit der Wand übereinstimmt. Diese Dinge faszinieren uns, erzeugen eine großar-

Zürich und München 1983), S. 20. ■ 3 Marc-Antoine Laugier, *Das Manifest des Klassizismus* (1753, Verlag für Architektur, Zürich und München 1989), S. 24. ■ 4 Preston Scott Cohen, unveröffentlicher Text, vom Architekten zur Verfügung gestellt. ■ 5 Mimi Moncier, unveröffentlicher Text, von der Künstlerin zur Verfügung gestellt.

Bildlegenden

Abb. 1: Louis Kahn, Bibliothek in Exeter, 1972. Foto: Doug Dolezal. ■ Abb. 2: Carlo Scarpa, Palazzo Querini Stampalia, Venedig, 1963. Foto: Eric Höweler. ■ Abb. 3–4: Diller + Scofidio, Eyebeam Building, New York, 2002. Fotos der Architeken. ■ Abb. 5: Preston Scott Cohen, Torus House, 1999. Fotos der Architekten. ■ Abb. 6:. Gordon Matta-Clark, „Four Corners", 1974. Foto: Estate of Gordon Matta-Clark / Artists' Rights Society (ARS), New York. ■ Abb. 7: Donald Judd, 100 Werke ohne Titel aus Aluminium, 1982–1986. Ständige Installation der Chinati Foundation, Marfa, Texas. Foto: Florian Holzherr. ■ Abb. 8: Donald Judd, Werke ohne Titel aus Beton, 1980–1984. Ständige Installation der Chinati Foundation. Foto: Florian Holzherr. Judd Art © Judd Foundation. ■ Abb. 9: Mimi Moncier, „My Lunch", 2002. Foto der Künstlerin. ■ Abb. 10: Andrea Palladio, *Die Vier Bücher zur Architektur*, s. Anm. 2. ■ Abb. 11: Patkau Architects, Wohnhaus in Vancouver, 2002. Foto: Paul Warchol.

Eléments hybrides

L'une des œuvres iconiques de l'architecture du XXe siècle se caractérise par sa rambarde située au sommet des escaliers et faisant également office de siège. Sa forme est celle d'une rampe, mais elle se transforme en un profil continu qui rappelle la forme humaine, sans différenciation entre le dossier du siège et la balustrade (ill. 1), telle une simple extension indissociable qui contredirait sa dualité. ■ L'incontestabilité d'une telle dualité s'est dégagée au fur et à mesure que ce livre a vu le jour. Telle qu'elle était conçue au départ, cette série devait être une liste d'éléments architecturaux, parties d'un bâtiment fonctionnellement pures et identifiables. Ce livre était censé être un catalogue à petite échelle d'éléments de notre époque, un index général des types d'éléments représentant la diversité de la pratique contemporaine. ■ Cependant, en nous plongeant dans trois décennies de photographies dans les archives de Paul Warchol, nous avons rapidement réalisé que la plupart des éléments ne se laisseraient pas classer dans des catégories claires. De nos jours, les éléments ne doivent plus autant être purs, irréductibles ou même identifiables. Tout aussi attrayante que cette idée ait pu être, il était clair que l'architecture d'aujourd'hui serait mieux représentée en mettant l'accent sur les éléments qui excluraient une structure de catalogue. ■ L'idée même de l'élément en tant que composant architectural irréductible provient de publications sur l'architecture. Les ouvrages les plus influents, écrits par Vitruvius et Palladio, sont des catalogues d'éléments, le vocabulaire essentiel du langage classique. Vitruvius a classifié les archétypes de temples et décrit trois ordres qu'il percevait comme des « formes élémentaires »

cifiques menant à une grossière standardisation du détail. ■ Dans les cas extrêmes, le tout n'est créé qu'en combinant ces éléments fixes de nouvelles manières. Cela limite le potentiel d'invention et étouffe la réflexion sur la nature des éléments mêmes. ■ Nous espérons que ce livre sera un tremplin stimulant la conception créatrice des éléments. Si le classicisme est une quête de « lois fixes et immuables »[3], nous examinons une nouvelle statégie dans les œuvres contemporaine qui explore les conflits, les divergences et les tensions dans l'architecture. ■ Alors que se développait le modernisme, les éléments sont restés au centre expressif de la « nouvelle époque » et de sa recherche de nouvelles formes. Et pourtant, les nouvelles idées modernistes réécrivent la définition des éléments. De nouvelles conceptions de l'espace sont apparues dans les peintures cubistes de Braque ou de Picasso, où les objets étaient simultanément représentés sous multiples points de vue. Cela a permis aux architectes de changer la manière dont fonctionnaient les éléments: Un panneau de verre faisant office de porte ou un toit servant également de jardin. ■ Le mouvement moderne, qui connaît un nouvel essor, a effectué une mutation unique des éléments conjoints en hybrides, combinant de nouveau plusieurs éléments, mais se débarrassant de l'identité des composants en faveur de l'indivisibilité du tout. Des tensions demeurent dans les relations entre les éléments, désormais intrinsèquement entremêlés dans une illusion semblable à un tableau d'Escher d'imbrications, de discordes et de stratification et bien plus complexe que les formes types du classicisme. La définition même des éléments s'assouplit, créant un potentiel pour les architectes de réaliser de nouvelles formes et

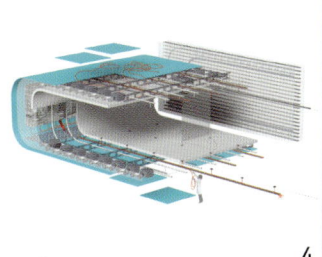

devant être arrangées en fonction de coutumes spécifiques, de manière à ce que « les parties distinctes et l'ensemble de la décoration s'harmonisent dans leurs proportions et dans leur symétrie. »[1] Il insiste sur la codification fixe et prédéterminée des éléments dans le classicisme. ■ Palladio a commencé par décrire les composants qui constituent un bâtiment, à partir de ses fondations et de ses murs, ses colonnes, ses pièces, ses sols et ses plafonds, ses cheminées, ses escaliers (ill. 10) et ses toits. La séquence suit la manière dont un bâtiment est assemblé et souligne donc la relation entre tout élément et la structure dans son ensemble, où « chaque partie ou membre est bien à sa place. »[2] L'accent est de nouveau mis sur l'« accord » entre les parties et les conventions. ■ Cette tradition a longtemps perduré. Aujourd'hui encore, nous constatons une conception classique dans deux camps idéologiques distincts. L'un traite les éléments comme des formes reproductibles où les détails identiques se répètent de projet en projet. L'autre promeut les grandes lignes normatives et contraignantes. Un phénomène d'autant plus répandu est la dépendance dans toute l'industrie à quelques sources spé-

d'exprimer de nouvelles manières d'utiliser les espaces. ■ Deux modèles informatiques récents, non construits et d'avant-garde, mettent l'accent sur l'essence d'un bâtiment. Dans une maquette d'Elizabeth Diller et de Ricardo Scofidio, designers célèbres pour fusionner les médias, l'intégralité du bâtiment est formée d'un ruban continu à deux fils qui se dissout en une surface ondoyante intacte contenant les systèmes de support entre ses deux couches (ill. 3–4). Le noyau crée des espaces qui encouragent les étudiants et le personnel à se mélanger avec les observateurs. Les architectes soulignent la capacité de l'élément à revendiquer des effets sociaux. ■ À moindre échelle, la Torus House de Preston Scott Cohen a un noyau tout aussi complexe (ill. 5), situé conventionnellement au centre de la maison, séparant les espaces de vie et reliant un garage à un toit en terrasse mais possédant des attributs indéterminés : est-ce une cage d'escalier, une cour intérieur, un puits de lumière, ou tout ceci à la fois ? Cela rajoute à la complexité de notre première lecture du noyau en tant qu'élément, en tant qu'objet toujours identifiable mais dont le bord se fond avec le plafond et le sol pour faire partie de la surface l'entourant. Les différentes formes du noyau sont « indivisibles par rapport au tout. »[4] ■ Les architectes défient les conventions démodées, soulevant le doute quant au caractère irréductible des éléments. Ils ouvrent ainsi la voie à de nouvelles réflexions, expérimentations, controverses ou même surprises qui s'opposent aux définitions restrictives des formes types. ■ Nous aimerions ajouter un dernier terme. De la même manière que les éléments façonnent l'architecture autour d'eux, la perception que nous avons d'eux est façonnée par des facteurs extérieurs. Les éléments communiquent souvent au travers d'un espace, créant des moments d'expression qui forment ensemble un argument plus complet. Bien que ce processus se produise également dans le classicisme ou l'œuvre de Scarpa, le discours contemporain a renforcé l'influence des facteurs extérieurs sur notre conception des éléments. L'œuvre « Four Corners » de Gordon Matta-Clark remet dans le contexte les fragments génériques d'un toit et de murs (ill. 6), s'interrogeant si l'élément lui-même est porteur de sens ou son contexte. Les travaux de Donald Judd à Marfa peuvent-ils être conçus comme œuvres individuelles sans le reste de la collection ou le site les entourant (ill. 7–8) ? Les facteurs contextuels ne sont pas simplement spatiaux, mais matériaux, impalpables, sociaux, etc. La lumière, les réflexions, le comportement, les méthodes de production, tout cela contribue au pouvoir de l'élément d'exprimer des idées. Le talent artistique se manifeste tout autant à l'extérieur qu'à l'intérieur de l'élément. ■ les méthodes de production, tout cela contribue au pouvoir de l'élément d'exprimer des idées. Le talent artistique se manifeste tout autant à l'extérieur qu'à l'intérieur de l'élément. ■ Les méthodes de production, tout cela contri-

sont de petites parties d'un bâtiment, mais ils portent un poids conceptuel énorme, imprégnés de beauté transcendante, de poésie, de subversion, de contradiction, de narration ou de tension. De tels éléments offrent une récompense dans les petits moments, permettant de découvrir de l'art dans les composants architecturaux de tous les jours. ■ Ils sont signes de la paternité de l'architecte, et ils forment la base d'une conversation directe entre le designer et l'observateur, leur but étant de réveiller quelque chose de sensuel en nous. ■ Les peintures de Mimi Moncier sont ainsi des catalogues des choses variées qui l'entourent dans son environnement immédiat (ill. 9). Dans ses tableaux, elle crée des figures qui « agissent en tant que dispositifs attirant l'attention » et qui invitent le regard « à contempler les couleurs comme des objets de désir »[5]. ■ Nous l'avons traité ce livre comme un catalogue de genres, un catalogue qui possède peut-être davantage les qualités opportunistes et pluralistes d'un album et qui insiste de manière moins rigide sur l'uniformité et l'absolutisme. Nous avons organisé les projets en catégories que nous considérons comme des jauges servant à mesurer l'innovation, la créativité et la complexité des détails présentés ici. Là où ils s'éloignent de ce système, expriment leur singularité, résistent à une catégorisation, voilà le moment déterminant qui les rend dignes de notre admiration.

Notes

1. Vitruvius, The Ten Books on Architecture (New York : Dover Publications, 1960), p. 75. ■ 2. Andrea Palladio, The Four Books of Architecture (New York : Dover Publications, 1965), p. 1. ■ 3. Marc-Antoine Laugier, An Essay on Architecture (Los Angeles : Hennessey & Ingalls, 1977), p. 3. ■ 4. Preston Scott Cohen, texte non publié mis à disposition par l'architecte. ■ 5. Mimi Moncier, déclaration non publiée mise à disposition par l'artiste.

bue au pouvoir de l'élément d'exprimer des idées. Le talent artistique se manifeste tout autant à l'extérieur qu'à l'intérieur de l'élément. ■ Tout cela se produit dans les œuvres décrites dans ce livre, des projets qui défient les termes des éléments. Une lucarne sert de piscine (ill. 11, p. 94–97) ; une colonne de métal enlace un banc de bois (p. 74–75) si bien que le dossier du siège abrite son occupant de même qu'il exprime le poids structurel du volume en porte-à-faux de la maison ; des étagères sont formées par des tiroirs qui dépassent mais qui peuvent être repoussés pour créer un solide mur de bois (p. 182–183) – le détail en changement perpétuel. Des boîtes à vêtements en bois sont dénuées de toute référence et reconstituées de manière abstraite (p. 4–5), ressemblant ainsi davantage à des objets minimalistes de Donald Judd qu'à des étalages ; une chapelle est dotée d'une paire de portes qui sont les composants continus de la façade (p. 20–23), les fenêtres ovales décrivant un motif sensible non pas aux portes mais au mur. Ces choses nous intoxiquent, brassant un délire de détails qui enrichit nos expériences de chaque environnement architectural. ■ Comme pour de nombreux détails de ce livre, ces éléments

Légendes

Illustration 1 : Louis Kahn, Exeter Library, 1972, avec l'aimable autorisation de Doug Dolezal. ■ Illustration 2 : Carlo Scarpa, Palazzo Querini Stampalia, 1963, avec l'aimable autorisation d'Eric Höweler. ■ Illustrations 3–4 : Diller + Scofidio, Eyebeam Building, New York, 2002, avec l'aimable autorisation des architectes. ■ Illustration 5 : Preston Scott Cohen, Torus House, 1999, avec l'aimable autorisation de l'architecte. ■ Illustration 6 : Gordon Matta-Clark, « Four Corners », 1974 ; photographie © 2002 Estate of Gordon Matta-Clark/Artists Rights Society (ARS), New York. ■ Illustration 7 : Donald Judd, 100 œuvres sans nom en aluminium, 1982–1986. Collection permanente de la Fondation Chinati, Marfa, Texas. Photographie de Florian Holzherr. Judd art © Judd Foundation. ■ Illustration 8 : Donald Judd, œuvre sans nom en béton, 1980–1984. Collection permanente de la Fondation Chinati, Marfa, Texas. Photographie de Florian Holzherr. Judd art © Judd Foundation. ■ Illustration 9 : Mimi Moncier, « My Lunch », 2002, avec l'aimable autorisation de l'artiste. ■ Illustration 10 : Andrea Palladio, The Four Books of Architecture (New York : Dover Publications, 1965). ■ Illustration 11 : Patkau Architects, maison de Vancouver, 2002. Photo de Paul Warchol.

Hybride vormen

In een iconisch werk van de 20e-eeuwse architectuur dient de trapleuning boven aan de trap ook als zitplaats. Zijn vorm past bij de trapleuning, maar vloeit over in een doorlopend profiel dat aansluit bij de menselijke contouren, zonder onderscheid tussen de rugleuning en de trapleuning (fig. 1), als een ondeelbare samensmelting die zijn dualiteit ontkent. ■ Dezelfde dualiteit openbaarde zich toen we dit boek maakten. In eerste instantie was het bedoeld als een lijst van architecturale elementen: kwantificeerbare en invariabele architecturale vormen, basiseenheden, puur functionele en herkenbare delen van een gebouw. Het moest een catalogus worden van moderne kleinschalige elementen, geen uitputtend naslagwerk, maar een algemeen overzicht van de soorten elementen in de diversiteit van de hedendaagse praktijk. ■ Tijdens het doorzoeken van dertig jaar foto's uit het archief van Paul Warchol beseften we echter dat veel elementen zich niet lieten categoriseren: een trappenhuis kon ook dienen als een lichtschacht, een wand en een vloer konden in elkaar overlopen en onscheidbaar zijn. Nu zijn de elementen minder puur en invariabel en soms zelfs minder herkenbaar. De moderne architecturale elementen zouden beter tot hun recht komen door juist die elementen te benadrukken die een categoriale indeling uitsloten. We konden de geschiedenis niet negeren. ■ Het idee van het element als een invariabele component is ontstaan uit publicaties over architectuur. De meest invloedrijke, die van Vitruvius en Palladio, zijn lijsten met elementen, een basisvocabulaire om het klassieke idioom. Vitruvius rubriceerde archetypische tempels en beschreef drie bouworden, die hij zag als 'elementaire vormen' die moesten worden gerang-

nieuwe manieren te combineren. Dit beperkt de vindingrijkheid en verstikt het denken over de aard van de elementen. ■ We hopen dat dit boek u uitdaagt om op een creatieve manier na te denken over elementen. Het classicisme is een zoektocht naar "onveranderlijke en vaststaande wetten"[3], maar wij onderzoeken een ideologie in het moderne werk die conflicten, onverenigbaarheid en spanningen in de architectuur verkent. Wij tonen elementen die de associaties die zijn toegeschreven aan typologische vormen, tegenspreken. Het is belangrijk om de moderne beweging te onderkennen. ■ Toen het modernisme zich ontwikkelde, bleven de elementen in het expressieve centrum van 'het nieuwe tijdperk' en zijn zoektocht naar nieuwe vormen. Toch gieten de modernistische ideeën de definitie van elementen in een nieuwe vorm. Nieuwe opvattingen over ruimte verschenen in de kubistische schilderijen van Braque en Picasso, waarin voorwerpen tegelijkertijd vanuit meerdere hoeken werden getoond. Hierdoor konden architecten de manier waarop elementen functioneerden veranderen. Ze konden worden verenigd in een samensmelting van delen: een glasplaat diende ook als deur, een dak functioneerde tevens als tuin. ■ Louis Kahn en Carlo Scarpa legden de delen open voor een creatieve verkenningsreis. Een werk van Scarpa heeft een deur zonder kozijn tussen muur en deurpaneel [fig. 2]. De muur is een verlenging van de deur en de deur loopt door in de muur. Deze visie schept een architecturale Minotaurus waarin elementen een nieuw geheel vormen, maar de delen nog zichtbaar zijn. ■ De revival van het modernisme heeft voor een verschuiving gezorgd van verenigde elementen naar hybriden, die eveneens een versmelting van verschillende elementen zijn, maar tevens de identiteit van de com-

schikt naar specifieke conventies opdat "de afzonderlijke delen en het hele ontwerp wat betreft verhouding en symmetrie zouden harmoniëren."[1] Hij legde de nadruk op de onveranderlijke en vooraf bepaalde codificatie van elementen in het classicisme. ■ Palladio beschreef eerst de componenten van een gebouw: fundering en muren, zuilen, kamers, vloeren en plafonds, schoorstenen, trappen (fig. 10) en daken. Daarna beschreef hij de samenstelling van een gebouw en benadrukte de relatie van elk element tot de grotere structuur, waarin "elk deel of lid zijn eigen plaats heeft."[2] Ook hier ligt het accent op het 'overeenstemmen' van de delen en de conventies. ■ Aan deze traditie is lang vastgehouden. Zelfs nu zien we een klassieke verstandhouding in twee verschillende ideologische kampen. Het ene kamp behandelt elementen als herhaalbare vormen, waarvan de identieke details bij elk project worden overgenomen. Het andere propageert bindende richtlijnen. Een wijder verspreid fenomeen is de afhankelijkheid van de hele bedrijfstak van een paar specifieke bronnen, wat leidt tot standaardisatie van details. ■ In het uiterste geval wordt het geheel slechts geschapen door deze onveranderlijke elementen op

ponenten opofferen aan de onscheidbaarheid van het geheel. Er blijven spanningen in de relatie tussen de elementen, die nu naadloos vervlochten zijn in een Escherachtige illusie van overlappingen, dissonanten en gelaagdheid die veel complexer is dan de basisvormen van het classicisme. De definitie van de elementen is minder strikt en daardoor kunnen architecten er creatiever mee omgaan, nieuwe vormen scheppen en ruimten anders benutten. ■ Twee onlangs gemaakte avant-gardistische computermodellen markeren de kern van een gebouw. In een plan van Elizabeth Diller en Ricardo Scofidio, ontwerpers die bekendstaan om het doen samensmelten van kunstvormen, bestaat het hele gebouw uit een doorlopend, tweelaags lint, dat overgaat in een ononderbroken golvend oppervlak; tussen de twee lagen liggen de bedrijfsinstallaties (fig. 3–4). De kern is hier een element dat de interactie tussen kunst en kunstvormen uitdrukt, en de ruimten zijn zo gemaakt dat ze contact tussen studenten, medewerkers en bezoekers stimuleren. De architecten benadrukken dat een element sociale effecten kan hebben. ■ Op kleinere schaal heeft het Torushuis van Preston Scott Cohen een net zo complexe kern (fig. 5), die zich zoals gebruikelijk in het midden van het huis bevindt, de woonruimten verdeelt en een carport verbindt met een dakterras, maar met onbestemde kenmerken: is het een trap, een binnenplaats, een lichtbron, of dit allemaal? Dit maakt onze eerste interpretatie van de kern als één stuk complex; het is nog steeds een herkenbaar object, maar gaat over in plafond en vloer en wordt zo een deel van het oppervlak eromheen. De vele gedaanten van de kern zijn "ondeelbaar gemaakt van het geheel."[4] ■ Dit getuigt van een experimentele vormverandering. Architecten tarten de afgezaagde conventies en trekken zowel de elementen als de invariabele vormen in twijfel. Dit opent, anders dan de beperkende definities van de vormen, deuren naar het nieuwe denken, experimenten, standpunten of verrassing. ■ Daar elementen de architectuur rondom hen vorm geven, is ons beeld ervan gevormd door uiterlijke factoren. Elementen staan dwars over een ruimte met elkaar in verbinding, afzonderlijke eenheden van expressie die samen een completer hoofdonderwerp vormen. Hoewel dit proces zich ook voordoet in het classicisme of in het werk van Scarpa, is de invloed van externe factoren op onze opvattingen over elementen nu groter geworden. In 'Four Corners' plaatst Gordon Matta-Clark de generieke delen van een dak en muren (fig. 6) in een andere context om te onderzoeken of het element zelf of zijn context betekenis heeft. Zijn Donald Judds werken in Marfa te begrijpen als individuele stukken zonder de rest van de collectie of de omgeving (fig. 7–8)? Contextuele factoren zijn niet eenvoudig ruimtelijk, maar materieel, etherisch, sociaal enzovoort. Licht, reflectie, gedrag en productiemethoden dragen bij aan de uitdrukkingskracht van een element. De artisticiteit ligt evenzeer

aardse schoonheid, poëzie, subversie, tegenstrijdigheid, vertelkunst en spanning. Zulke elementen belonen soms; het ontdekken van kunst in de alledaagse componenten van de architectuur. Ze getuigen van de ideeën van de architect en vormen de basis van een rechtstreekse conversatie tussen de ontwerper en de toeschouwer, en het is de bedoeling dat ze iets in ons losmaken. ■ De schilderijen van Mimi Moncier zijn bijvoorbeeld catalogi van de dingen rondom haar, haar directe omgeving (fig. 9). In haar schilderijen zien we geringde figuren met diepe kleuren, die "fungeren als aandachttrekkers" die de ogen uitnodigen "om naar de kleuren te kijken als voorwerpen van begeerte."[5] Dat hopen we met dit boek ook te bereiken: dat u zich overgeeft aan deze voorwerpen. ■ Dit boek is een catalogus van soorten geworden. Een catalogus die misschien eerder getuigt van de opportunistische en pluralistische eigenschappen van een plakboek, dan van een star vasthouden aan consistentie en absolutisme. We hebben de projecten gerangschikt in categorieën die wij zien als criteria om de vernieuwing, creativiteit en de complexiteit van de hier getoonde details te bepalen. Waar ze van dit systeem afdwalen, hun uniciteit tonen, weigeren zich te laten categoriseren, is juist dat bepalend, daardoor verdienen ze onze bewondering.

Noten

1. Vitruvius, *The Ten Books on Architecture* (New York: Dover Publications, 1960), 75. ■ 2. Andrea Palladio, *The Four Books of Architecture* (New York: Dover Publications, 1965), 1. ■ 3. Marc-Antoine Laugier, *An Essay on Architecture* (Los Angeles: Hennessey & Ingalls, 1977), 3. ■ 4. Preston Scott Cohen, niet-gepubliceerde tekst ter beschikking gesteld door de architect. ■ 5. Mimi Moncier, niet-gepubliceerde verklaring ter beschikking gesteld door de architect.

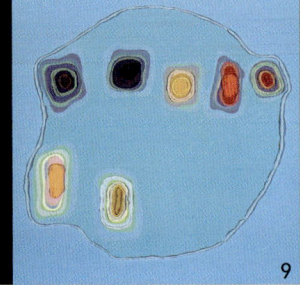

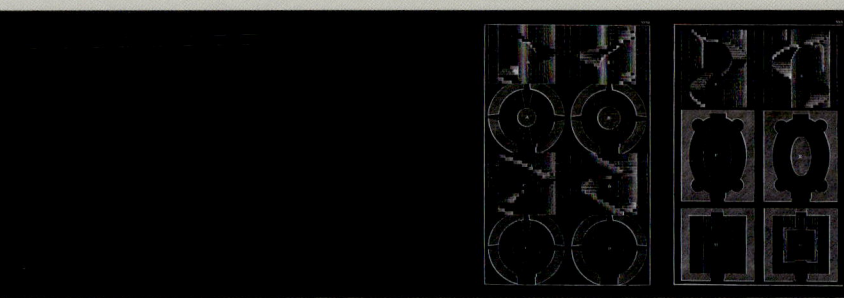

buiten als binnen het element. ■ Dit alles zien we in de hier getoonde werken, projecten die de definitie van elementen uitdagen. Een dakraam is tevens een zwembad (fig. 11, blz. 94–97); een metalen zuil is vervlochten met een houten bank (blz. 74–75) zodat de rugleuning degene die op de bank zit beschut en tevens het gewicht van de vrijdragende constructie uitdrukt; een idee van planken wordt gevormd door uitspringende laden die terug kunnen schuiven en dan een stevige houten muur vormen (blz. 182–183), het detail verandert voortdurend; houten kledingkasten zijn ontdaan van alles wat op hun functie duidt en opnieuw samengesteld door abstractie (blz. 4–5) zodat ze meer lijken op minimalistische stukken van Donald Judd dan op uitstalkasten voor een winkel; een kapel heeft deuren die doorlopende componenten van de gevel zijn (blz. 20–23), ovale ramen beschrijven een patroon dat niet harmonieert met de deuren, maar met de muur. Deze zaken bedwelmen ons, ze brouwen een delirium van details dat onze ervaring van elke architecturale omgeving verrijkt. ■ Zoals bij veel details in dit boek zijn deze elementen kleine delen van een gebouw, maar hebben ze een enorme conceptuele betekenis, doortrokken van boven-

Fotobijschriften

Figuur 1: Louis Kahn, Exeter Library, 1972; illustratie beschikbaar gesteld door Doug Dolezal. ■ Figuur 2: Carlo Scarpa, Palazzo Querini Stampalia, 1963; illustratie beschikbaar gesteld door Eric Höweler. ■ Figuren 3-4: Diller + Scofidio, Eyebeam Building, New York, 2002; illustraties beschikbaar gesteld door de architecten. ■ Figuur 5: Preston Scott Cohen, Torus House, 1999; illustratie beschikbaar gesteld door de architect. ■ Figuur 6: Gordon Matta-Clark, 'Four Corners', 1974; illustratie © 2002 Estate of Gordon Matta-Clark/Artists Rights Society (ARS), New York. ■ Figuur 7: Donald Judd, 100 werken in gewalst aluminium, zonder titel, 1982–1986. Chinati Foundation permanente collectie, Marfa, Texas. Fotografie Florian Holzherr. Judd art © Judd Foundation. ■ Figuur 8: Donald Judd, werk in beton, zonder titel, 1980–1984. Chinati Foundation permanente collectie, Marfa, Texas. Fotografie Florian Holzherr. Judd art © Judd Foundation. ■ Figuur 9: Mimi Moncier, 'My Lunch', 2002; illustratie beschikbaar gesteld door de kunstenaar. ■ Figuur 10: Andrea Palladio, *The Four Books of Architecture* (New York: Dover Publications, 1965). ■ Figuur 11: Patkau Architects, Vancouver House, 2002; illustratie Paul Warchol.

türen portes deuren

VORHERIGE DOPPELSEITE: Architecture Research Office, Büros der Firma Capital Z, New York, 1998. VORLIEGENDE DOPPELSEITE: Pasanella + Klein Stolzman + Berg Architects, Wohnung in der Fifth Avenue, New York, 1989. Die metallgerahmten Türflächen sind so angeordnet, dass sie der Aussicht aus dem Apartment auf den Central Park Struktur verleihen.

PAGE PRÉCÉDENTE : Architecture Research Office, bureaux principaux de Capital Z, New York, 1998. CETTE DOUBLE PAGE : Pasanella + Klein Stolzman + Berg Architects, résidence sur Fifth Avenue, New York, 1989. Les vantaux encadrés de métal sont positionnés de manière à structurer les vues de l'appartement sur Central Park.

VORIGE BLADZIJDEN: Architecture Research Office, kantooren van de firma Capital Z, New York 1998. DEZE BLADZIJDEN: Pasanella + Klein Stolzman + Berg Architects, woning aan Fifth Avenue, New York, 1989. De in metalen lijsten gevatte deuren zijn zo ontworpen dat ze structuur geven aan het uitzicht op Central Park.

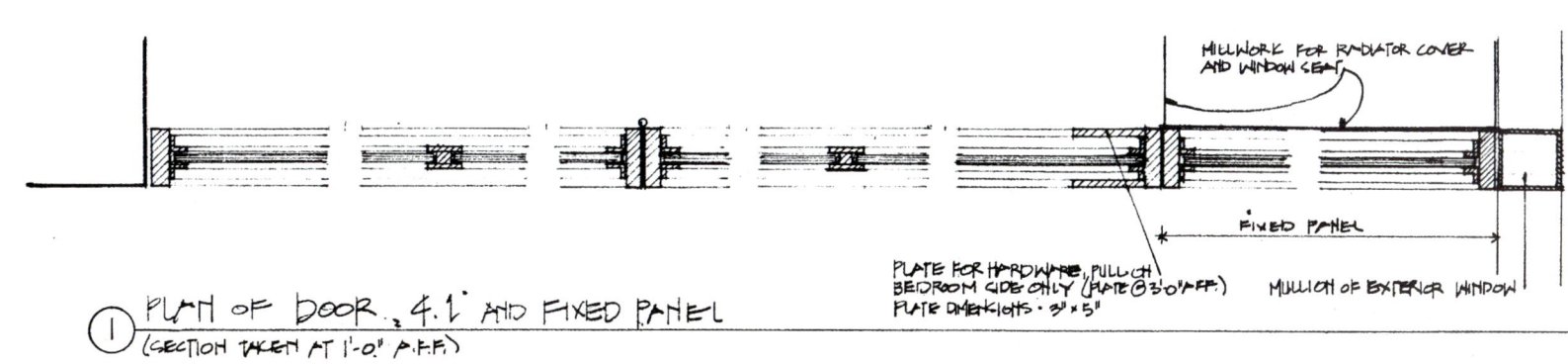

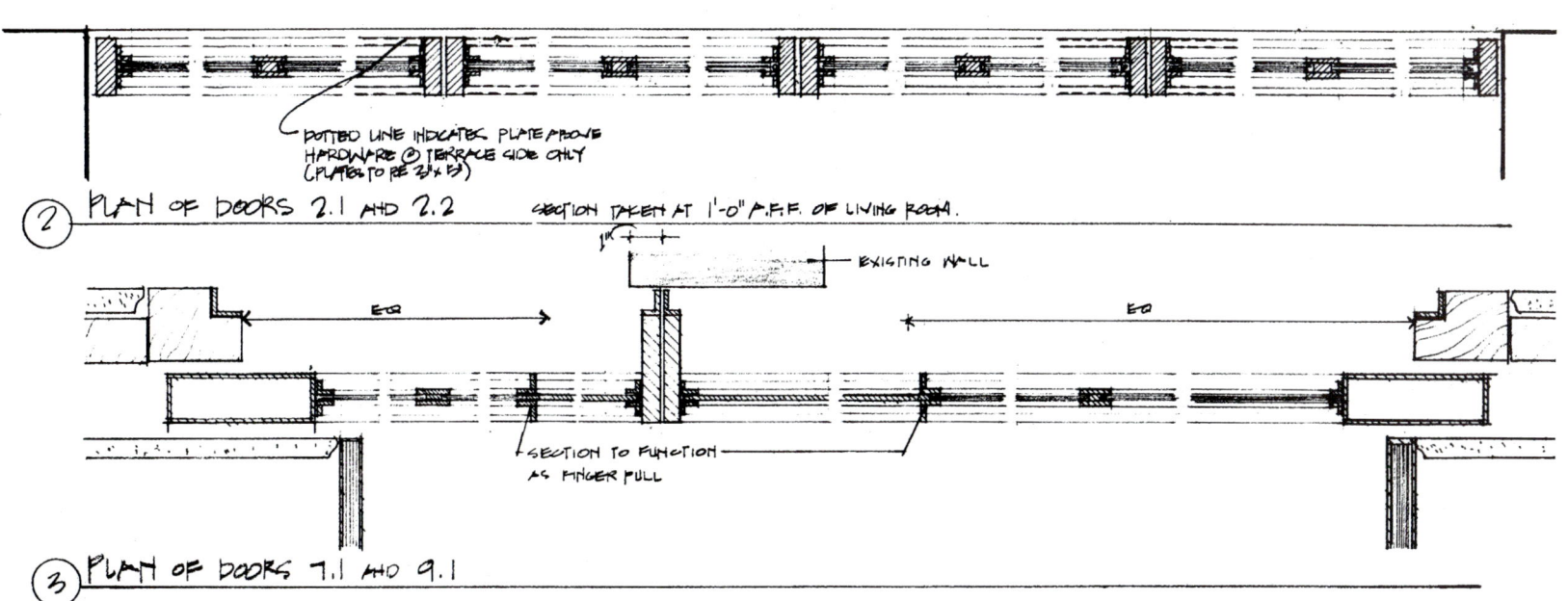

Maya Lin Studio/David Hotson Architect, Wohnhaus an der Upper East Side, New York, 1999. Drehbare Flügel verwischen den Unterschied zwischen Türen und Wänden. Der helle Farbton des Sykomorenfurniers bildet einen Kontrast zu den dunkleren Streifen auf den Böden und Wänden.

Maya Lin Studio/David Hotson Architect, résidence dans Upper East Side, New York, 1999. Les panneaux pivotants estompent la distinction entre les portes et les murs. La couleur claire des lambris plaqués de sycomore contraste avec les bandes plus sombres apposées le long des sols et des murs.

Maya Lin Studio/David Hotson Architect, Upper East Side Residence, New York, 1999. Draaipanelen laten het onderscheid tussen deuren en muren vervagen. De lichte kleur van het paneelwerk van esdoornfineer contrasteert met de donkere strepen op de vloeren en muren.

VORHERIGE DOPPELSEITE: Steven Holl Architects, Kapelle St. Ignatius, Seattle, 1997. Die handgeschnitzten gelben Türen aus Zedernholz werden durch Bronzegriffe hervorgehoben und sind von ovalen Fenstern unterschiedlicher Form und Größe durchbrochen. VORLIEGENDE DOPPELSEITE: Steven Holl Architects, Kapelle St. Ignatius, Seattle, 1997. Die Haupteingangstür an der Ecke liegt an einem spiegelnden Weiher. Durch die Platzierung der Kapelle ist ein neuer viereckiger Gebäudekomplex auf dem Campus entstanden.

DOUBLE PAGE PRÉCÉDENTE : Steven Holl Architects, chapelle St. Ignatius, Seattle, 1997. Les portes en cèdre jaune de l'Alaska travaillé à la gouge sont signalées par des poignées en bronze et décorées par des fenêtres ovales de différentes formes et tailles. CETTE DOUBLE PAGE : Steven Holl Architects, chapelle St. Ignatius, Seattle, 1997. La porte principale située à l'entrée d'angle fait face à un étang réfléchissant. La chapelle est orientée de façon à former un nouveau quadrangle sur le campus.

VORIGE BLADZIJDEN: Steven Holl Architects, Chapel of St. Ignatius, Seattle, 1997. Handgesneden Alaska-cederhouten deuren met markante bronzen grepen en ovale gaten van diverse vormen en afmetingen. DEZE BLADZIJDEN: Steven Holl Architects, Chapel of St. Ignatius, Seattle, 1997. De hoofddeur in de hoek weerspiegelt in de vijver. De kapel is zo geplaatst dat hij een nieuwe vierhoekige binnenplaats vormt.

Steven Holl Architects, Texas Stretto House, Dallas, 1992. Eine Eingangstür aus bewittertem Metall wird Teil einer geometrischen Komposition, die aus Glas und Außenplatten aus Beton besteht.

Steven Holl Architects, maison Stretto, Dallas, Texas, 1992. La porte d'entrée de métal prépatiné devient partie intégrante d'une composition géométrique comprenant également du verre et des panneaux extérieurs en béton.

Steven Holl Architects, Texas Stretto House, Dallas, 1992. De toegangsdeur van verweerd metaal maakt deel uit van een rechthoekige compositie waarin tevens glas en betonnen platen aan de buitenkant zijn opgenomen.

Craig Bassam Studio, Hauptverwaltung Bally Caslano, Schweiz, 2000. Dieser Korridor ist als Folge gleicher Tafeln konzipiert, einschließlich der Schiebetüren aus Eiche. Ein schlichtes, eingeschnittenes Detail am Türrand verweist auf Handwerk und Handarbeit und lenkt den Blick auf die Tür, wenn sie zurückgeschoben ist.

Craig Bassam Studio, siège de Bally Caslano, Suisse, 2000. Conçu comme une série de panneaux identiques comprenant les portes coulissantes en chêne. Le bord de la porte est orné d'un simple détail gravé qui suggère une intervention artistique et artisanale et donne à cette dernière un aspect différent en position ouverte.

Craig Bassam Studio, Bally Caslano Headquarters, Caslano, Zwitserland, 2000. De hele gang is vormgegeven door middel van gelijkvormige panelen waaronder eiken schuifdeuren. Een eenvoudig uitgesneden detail op de rand van de deur suggereert ambachtelijkheid en handwerk, en geeft aan waar de deur zit als hij open is.

fenster fenêtres ramen

VORHERIGE SEITE: Steven Holl Architects, Kapelle St. Ignatius, Seattle, 1997. VORLIEGENDE DOPPELSEITE: Brian Healy Architects (mit Michael Ryan), Haus am Strand, Loveladies, New Jersey, 1996. Eine Gruppe von vier Fenstern wird zum Teil einer geometrischen Fassadenkomposition, die auch einen überstehenden Sonnenschutz und den Versorgungskern einschließt.

PAGE PRÉCÉDENTE : Steven Holl Architects, chapelle St. Ignatius, Seattle, 1997. CETTE DOUBLE PAGE : Brian Healy Architects (avec Michael Ryan), maison de plage, Loveladies, New Jersey, 1997. Quatre groupements de fenêtres sont intégrés à la composition géométrique de la façade qui comprend également un auvent faisant office de parasol ainsi que le noyau de service de la maison.

VORIGE BLADZIJDE: Steven Holl Architects, Chapel of St. Ignatius, Seattle, 1997. DEZE BLADZIJDEN: Brian Healy Architects (met Michael Ryan), Beach House, Loveladies, New Jersey, 1996. De vier gegroepeerde ramen maken deel uit van de rechthoekige compositie van de gevel met zonwerende overhangende dakranden en de installatiekern van het huis.

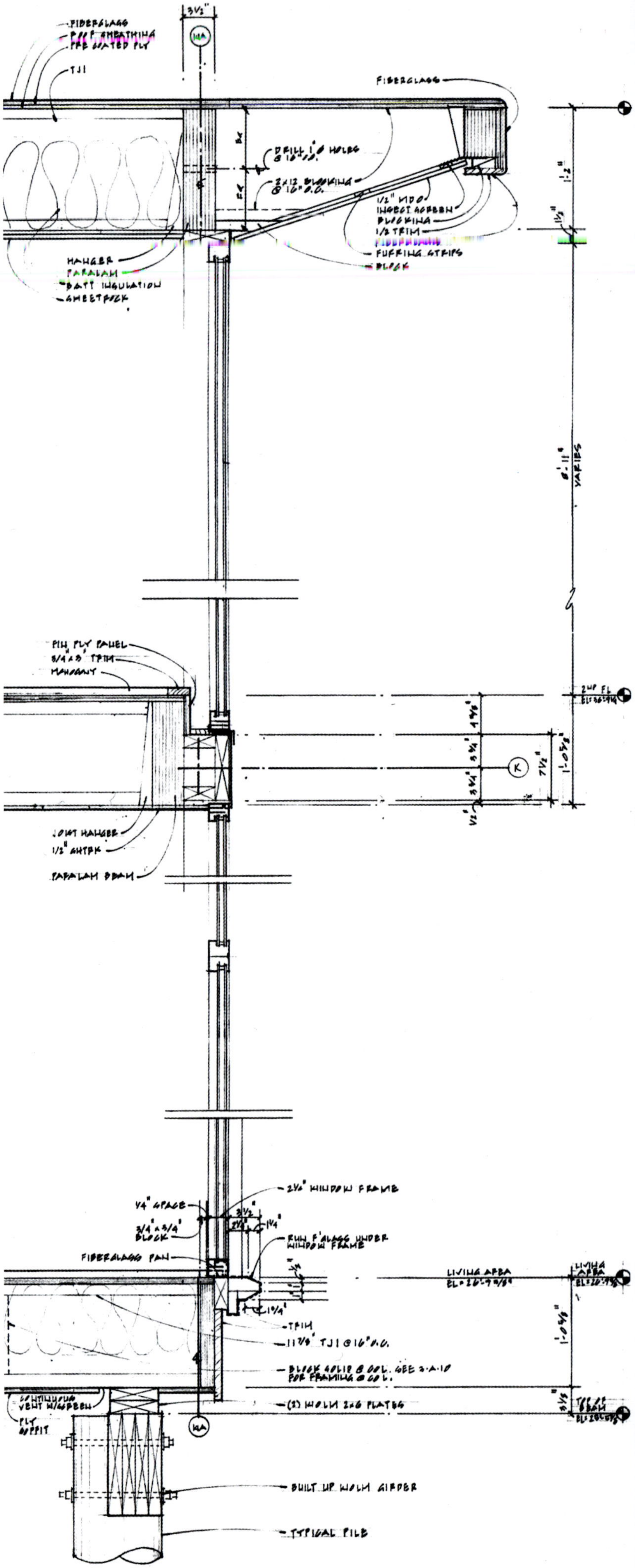

Maya Lin Studio/David Hotson Architect, Wohnhaus an der Upper East Side, New York, 1999. Die in natürliches Licht getauchte, doppelgeschosshohe Eingangshalle eines Stadthauses kann durch eine schwenkbare Klappe aus Sykomorenfurnier mit dem Schlafraum der Besitzer verbunden werden.

Maya Lin Studio/David Hotson Architect, résidence dans Upper East Side, New York, 1999. Dans une maison de ville, un hall d'entrée sur deux niveaux, baigné de lumière naturelle, s'ouvre sur la principale chambre à coucher par le biais d'un panneau pivotant en placage de sycomore.

Maya Lin Studio/David Hotson Architect, Upper East Side Residence, New York, 1999. De twee niveaus hoge hal in deze stadswoning is vol daglicht. Hij staat in verbinding met de ouderslaapkamer via een draaipaneel met esdoornfineer.

Steven Holl Architects, Y House, nördlich von New York, 1999. Die Flügel dieses Hauses stoßen in stumpfem Winkel aneinander; die zahlreichen Fenster sind so angeordnet, dass sie spezielle Ausblicke auf die Berge einrahmen, aber an den Innenwänden auch genügend Platz für Kunst lassen.

Steven Holl Architects, maison en Y, nord de New York, 1999. Les ailes de la maison se rejoignent à angle obtus, et les nombreuses fenêtres sont placées de manière à encadrer les remarquables vues sur les montagnes mais aussi à maximiser la quantité d'espace destiné à l'art sur les murs intérieurs.

Steven Holl Architects, Y House, Upstate New York, 1999. De vleugels van het huis raken elkaar in een stompe hoek. De vele ramen kaderen bijzondere uitzichten op de bergen in, maar zorgen binnen in het huis ook voor maximale wandruimte, die bestemd is voor kunstwerken.

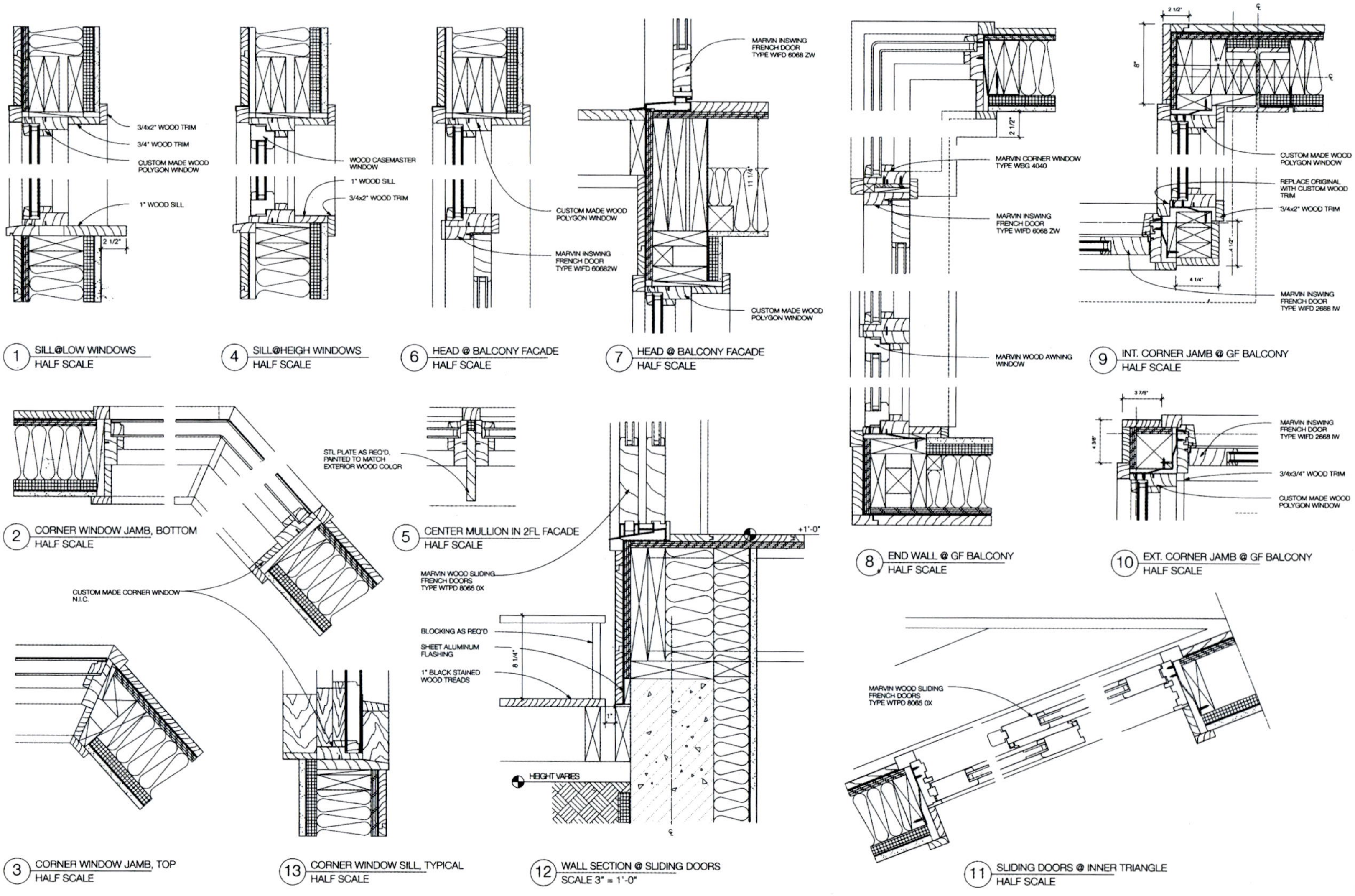

3/4x2" WOOD TRIM
3/4" WOOD TRIM
CUSTOM MADE WOOD POLYGON WINDOW
1" WOOD SILL
2 1/2"

① SILL@LOW WINDOWS — HALF SCALE

WOOD CASEMASTER WINDOW
1" WOOD SILL
3/4x2" WOOD TRIM

④ SILL@HEIGH WINDOWS — HALF SCALE

CUSTOM MADE WOOD POLYGON WINDOW
MARVIN INSWING FRENCH DOOR TYPE WIFD 60082W

⑥ HEAD @ BALCONY FACADE — HALF SCALE

MARVIN INSWING FRENCH DOOR TYPE WIFD 6068 ZW
11 1/4"
CUSTOM MADE WOOD POLYGON WINDOW
CUSTOM MADE WOOD POLYGON WINDOW

⑦ HEAD @ BALCONY FACADE — HALF SCALE

2 1/2"
2 1/2"
MARVIN CORNER WINDOW TYPE WBG 4040
MARVIN INSWING FRENCH DOOR TYPE WIFD 6068 ZW
MARVIN WOOD AWNING WINDOW

CUSTOM MADE WOOD POLYGON WINDOW
REPLACE ORIGINAL WITH CUSTOM WOOD TRIM
3/4x2" WOOD TRIM
4 1/4"
MARVIN INSWING FRENCH DOOR TYPE WIFD 2668 IW

⑨ INT. CORNER JAMB @ GF BALCONY — HALF SCALE

CUSTOM MADE CORNER WINDOW N.I.C.

② CORNER WINDOW JAMB, BOTTOM — HALF SCALE

STL PLATE AS REQ'D, PAINTED TO MATCH EXTERIOR WOOD COLOR

⑤ CENTER MULLION IN 2FL FACADE — HALF SCALE

MARVIN WOOD SLIDING FRENCH DOORS TYPE WTPD 8065 OX
BLOCKING AS REQ'D
SHEET ALUMINUM FLASHING
1" BLACK STAINED WOOD TREADS

⑧ END WALL @ GF BALCONY — HALF SCALE

3 7/8"
MARVIN INSWING FRENCH DOOR TYPE WIFD 2668 IW
3/4x3/4" WOOD TRIM
CUSTOM MADE WOOD POLYGON WINDOW

⑩ EXT. CORNER JAMB @ GF BALCONY — HALF SCALE

③ CORNER WINDOW JAMB, TOP — HALF SCALE

⑬ CORNER WINDOW SILL, TYPICAL — HALF SCALE

+1'-0"
HEIGHT VARIES

⑫ WALL SECTION @ SLIDING DOORS — SCALE 3" = 1'-0"

MARVIN WOOD SLIDING FRENCH DOORS TYPE WTPD 8065 OX

⑪ SLIDING DOORS @ INNER TRIANGLE — HALF SCALE

Steven Holl Architects, Texas Stretto House, Dallas, 1992. Die leichte Krümmung des Daches verleiht diesem Haus bei ansonsten orthogonaler Ausbildung der großen Glasfenster Formenvielfalt. FOLGENDE DOPPELSEITE: Steven Holl Architects, Bellevue Art Museum, Bellevue, Washington, 2001. Die drei unterschiedlichen Belichtungselemente des Museums sind durch ein innenliegendes, zum Teil durchscheinendes Fenster sichtbar.

Steven Holl Architects, maison Stretto, Dallas, Texas, 1992. L'arche du toit légèrement sphérique donne une variété angulaire à la composition sinon orthogonale des larges fenêtres en verre de la maison. DOUBLE PAGE SUIVANTE : Steven Holl Architects, Bellevue Art Museum, Bellevue, Washington, 2001. Les trois systèmes d'éclairage distincts du musée sont visibles par une fenêtre interne en partie translucide.

Steven Holl Architects, Texas Stretto House, Dallas, 1992. De zachte, sfeervolle welving van het dak zorgt voor afwisseling in de verder orthogonale compositie van de grote glasramen van het huis. VOLGENDE BLADZIJDEN: Steven Holl Architects, Bellevue Art Museum, Bellevue, Washington, 2001. De drie soorten verlichting van het museum zijn te zien door een gedeeltelijk doorschijnend binnenraam.

Steven Holl Architects, Cranbrook Institute of Science, Bloomfield Hills, Michigan, 1999. Eine neue Eingangshalle bildet ein „Lichtlaboratorium" mit einer nach Süden orientierten Wand aus verschiedenen Glastypen. An den Wänden der Lobby entstehen durch die Veränderung des Tageslichts unterschiedliche Lichtphänomene wie Strahlenbrechung und Spektralfarben.

Steven Holl Architects, Institut des sciences de Cranbrook, « Laboratoire de lumière » Bloomfield Hills, Michigan, 1999. Le dont le mur sud est composé de divers types de verre, forme le hall de réception. Les différents phénomènes de lumière tels que la réfraction et les couleurs prismatiques s'étalent sur les murs en fonction des changements de la lumière du soleil.

Steven Holl Architects, Cranbrook Institute of Science, Bloomfield Hills, Michigan, 1999. Een nieuwe hal bij de ingang vormt een 'Light Laboratory' met een muur op het zuiden van allerlei soorten glas. Op de muren tovert het zonlicht lichtverschijnselen zoals straalbreking en prismatische kleuren.

NBBJ, Büros der Firma Teledesic, Bellevue, Washington, 2000. In einem sanierten Industriebau fällt diffuses Licht von Norden durch große, gaubenähnliche Dachfenster – „Lichtmonitore" – und im Erdgeschoss durch Fensterelemente aus Klar- und Mattglas in die Räume.

NBBJ, bureaux Teledesic, Bellevue, Washington, 2000. Dans un bâtiment industriel rénové, de larges « moniteurs de lumière » semblables à des lucarnes et des éléments plus bas en verre clair et givré laissent entrer une lumière boréale diffuse dans les pièces.

NBBJ, Teledesic Offices, Bellevue, Washington, 2000. In een gerenoveerd industrieel pand zorgen grote dakkapelachtige 'lichtsluizen' en, een niveau lager, eenheden van helder en mat glas voor diffuus noordelijk licht in de vertrekken.

wände murs muren

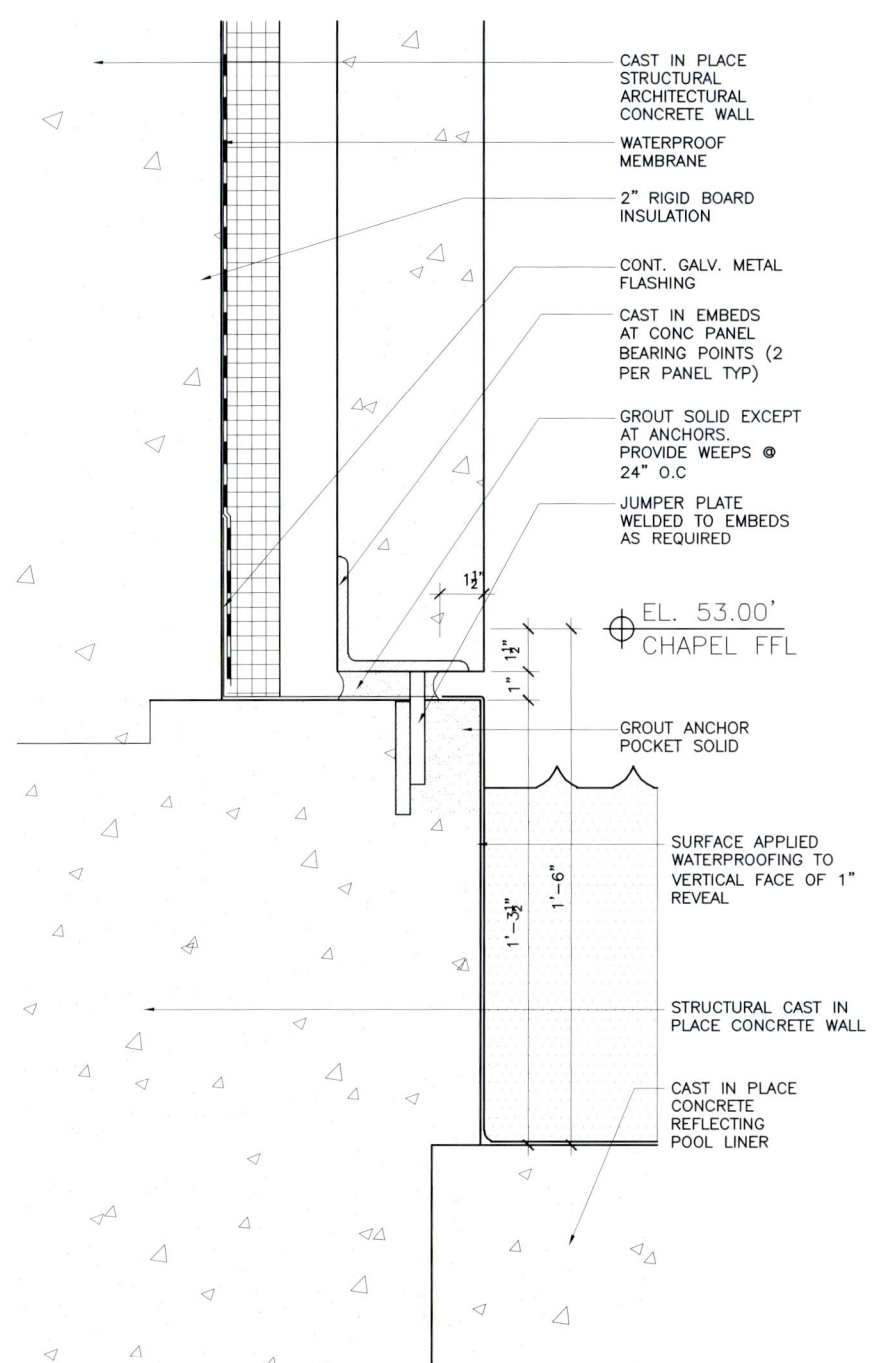

CAST IN PLACE
STRUCTURAL
ARCHITECTURAL
CONCRETE WALL

WATERPROOF
MEMBRANE

2" RIGID BOARD
INSULATION

CONT. GALV. METAL
FLASHING

CAST IN EMBEDS
AT CONC PANEL
BEARING POINTS (2
PER PANEL TYP)

GROUT SOLID EXCEPT
AT ANCHORS.
PROVIDE WEEPS @
24" O.C

JUMPER PLATE
WELDED TO EMBEDS
AS REQUIRED

⊕ EL. 53.00'
CHAPEL FFL

GROUT ANCHOR
POCKET SOLID

SURFACE APPLIED
WATERPROOFING TO
VERTICAL FACE OF 1"
REVEAL

STRUCTURAL CAST IN
PLACE CONCRETE WALL

CAST IN PLACE
CONCRETE
REFLECTING
POOL LINER

④ DETAIL PRECAST PANEL @ POOL

Steven Holl Architects, Bellevue Art Museum, Bellevue, Washington, 2001. Ein breites Band aus natürlichem und künstlichem Licht überzieht die gekrümmten Wände des Museums.

Steven Holl Architects, Bellevue Art Museum, Bellevue, Washington, 2001. Un mélange de lumière naturelle et artificielle baigne les murs curvilignes du musée.

Steven Holl Architects, Bellevue Art Museum, Bellevue, Washington, 2001. De welvende muren van het museum baden in daglicht en kunstlicht.

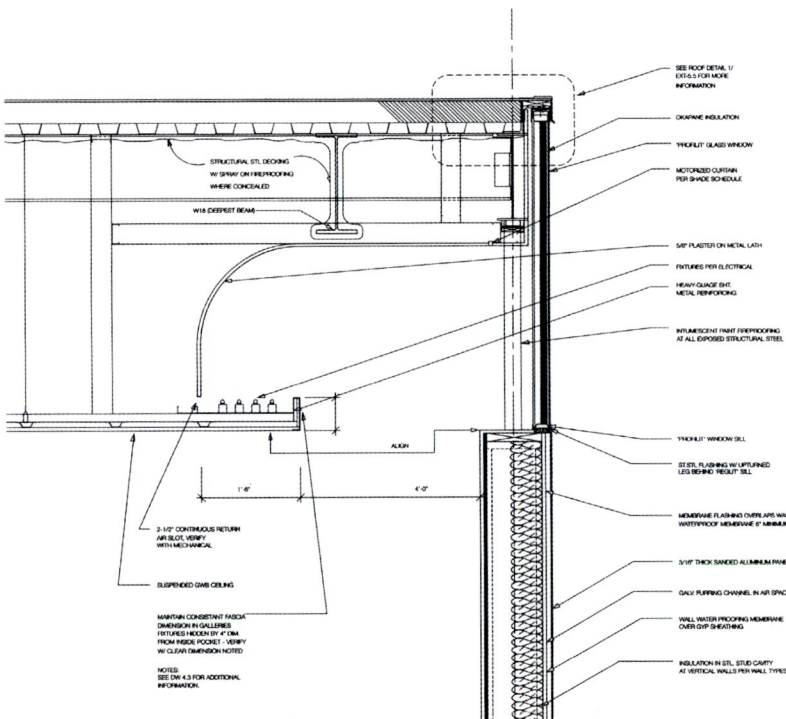

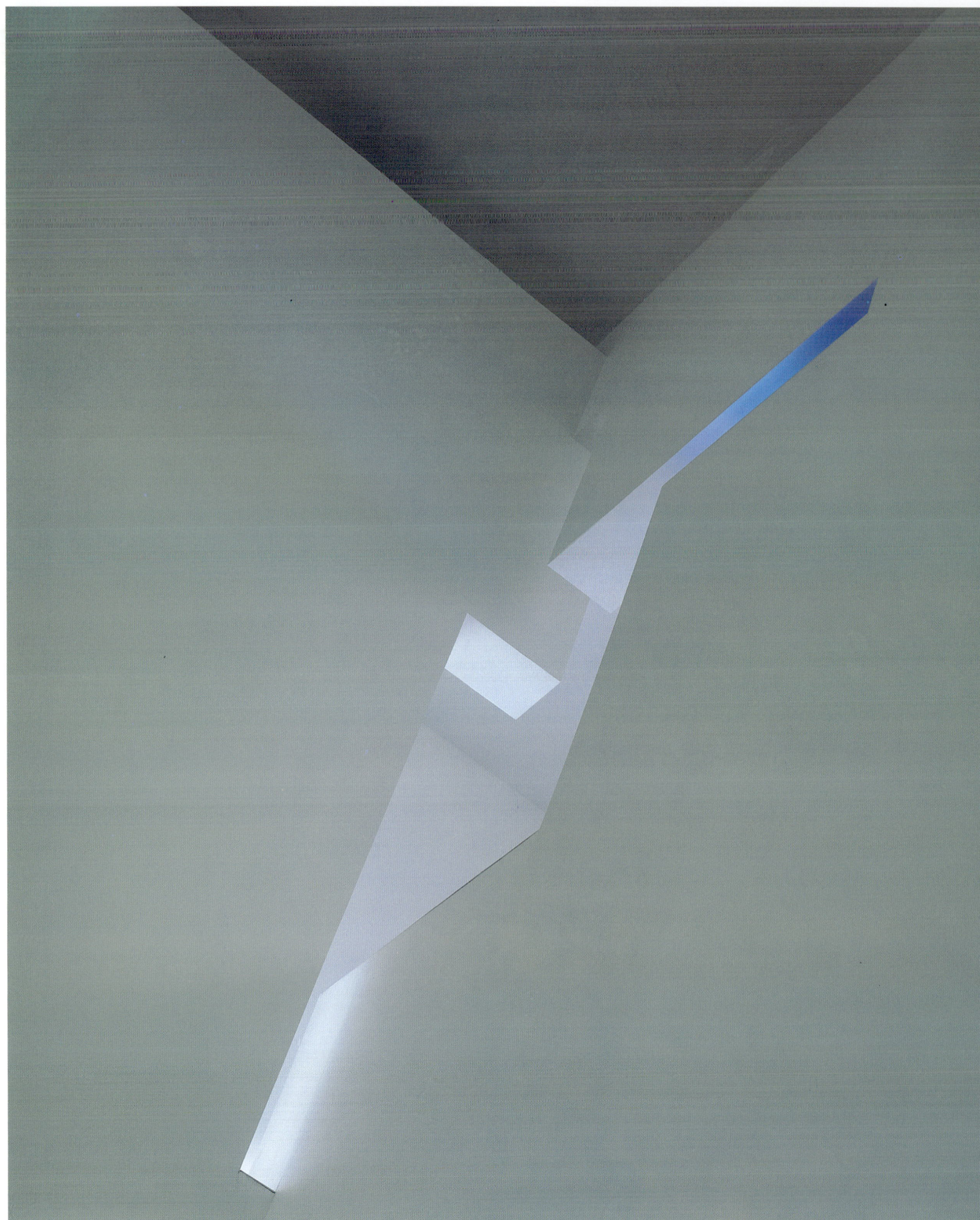

Steven Holl Architects, Büros der Firma D. E. Shaw & Co., New York, 1992. Der Eingangskubus von ca. 10 m Seitenlänge hat an wichtigen Punkten Einschnitte, auf deren Innenseiten sich farbiges Licht mit Sonnenlicht mischt und sich ständig wechselnde Überschneidungen von Farben und geometrische Volumen ergeben.

Steven Holl Architects, bureaux D. E. Shaw & Co., New York, 1992. L'entrée en forme de cube de plus de dix mètres porte des encoches en des points stratégiques, et des lumières colorées fixées à l'arrière ou au fond de ces orifices se mélangent à la lumière du soleil pour produire des croisements incessants de couleurs et de volumes géométriques.

Steven Holl Architects, D. E. Shaw & Co. Offices, New York, 1992. De kubus die de ingang vormt, is op strategische punten ingesneden. Gekleurd licht op de rug- en bodemvlakken van de inkepingen vermengt zich met zonlicht, waardoor een wisselend patroon van kleuren en geometrische vormen ontstaat.

Gluckman Mayner Architects, Mary Boone Gallery, New York, 1996. Alle sichtbaren Flächen sind aus Beton oder verputzt und in ähnlichem hellgrauen Ton gehalten. Dadurch werden die Unterschiede zwischen Wand, Boden und Decke verwischt. Die große, zentrale Stütze bildet eine starke, vertikale Achse in diesem vorwiegend horizontalen Raum.

Gluckman Mayner Architects, galerie Mary Boone, New York, 1996. Toutes les surfaces visibles sont en béton et en plâtre, de finition similaire et teintées de gris clair, produisant un effet qui estompe la limite entre le sol, le mur et le plafond. La large colonne centrale suggère un puissant axe vertical dans un espace à dominante horizontale.

Gluckmann Mayner Architects, Mary Boone Gallery, New York, 1996. Alle zichtbare oppervlakken zijn van beton en pleisterwerk, op dezelfde manier afgewerkt en lichtgrijs. Daardoor vervaagt het onderscheid tussen vloer, muur en plafond. De vergrote centrale zuil suggereert een sterke verticale as in een voornamelijk horizontale ruimte.

Smith-Miller + Hawkinson Architects, Privatwohnung, New York, 1997. Versetzbare Wände sind in unterschiedlichen Winkeln angeordnet und ermöglichen eine schnelle Umgestaltung dieses Lofts mit hoher Decke. FOLGENDE DOPPELSEITE: Deborah Berke & Partners, Wohnung Howell (Loft), New York, 1999. Öffnung und Einfassung eines Kamins bilden eine schlichte geometrische Komposition an einer nackten Putzwand.

Smith-Miller + Hawkinson Architects, résidence privée, New York, 1997. Les cloisons mobiles sont placées à angles variés, ce qui permet de rapidement reconfigurer un espace de loft à plafond haut. DOUBLE PAGE SUIVANTE : Deborah Berke & Partners, loft Howell, New York, 1999. L'ouverture destinée à la cheminée et à sa tablette forme une composition géométrique simple sur le sobre mur de plâtre.

Smith-Miller + Hawkinson Architects, Private Residence, New York, 1997. Dankzij beweegbare muren kan de bovenverdieping met het hoge plafond snel worden veranderd. VOLGENDE BLADZIJDEN: Deborah Berke & Partners, Howell Loft, New York, 1999. De opening voor een haard en een mantel is een simpele rechthoekige compositie in een extra gipswand.

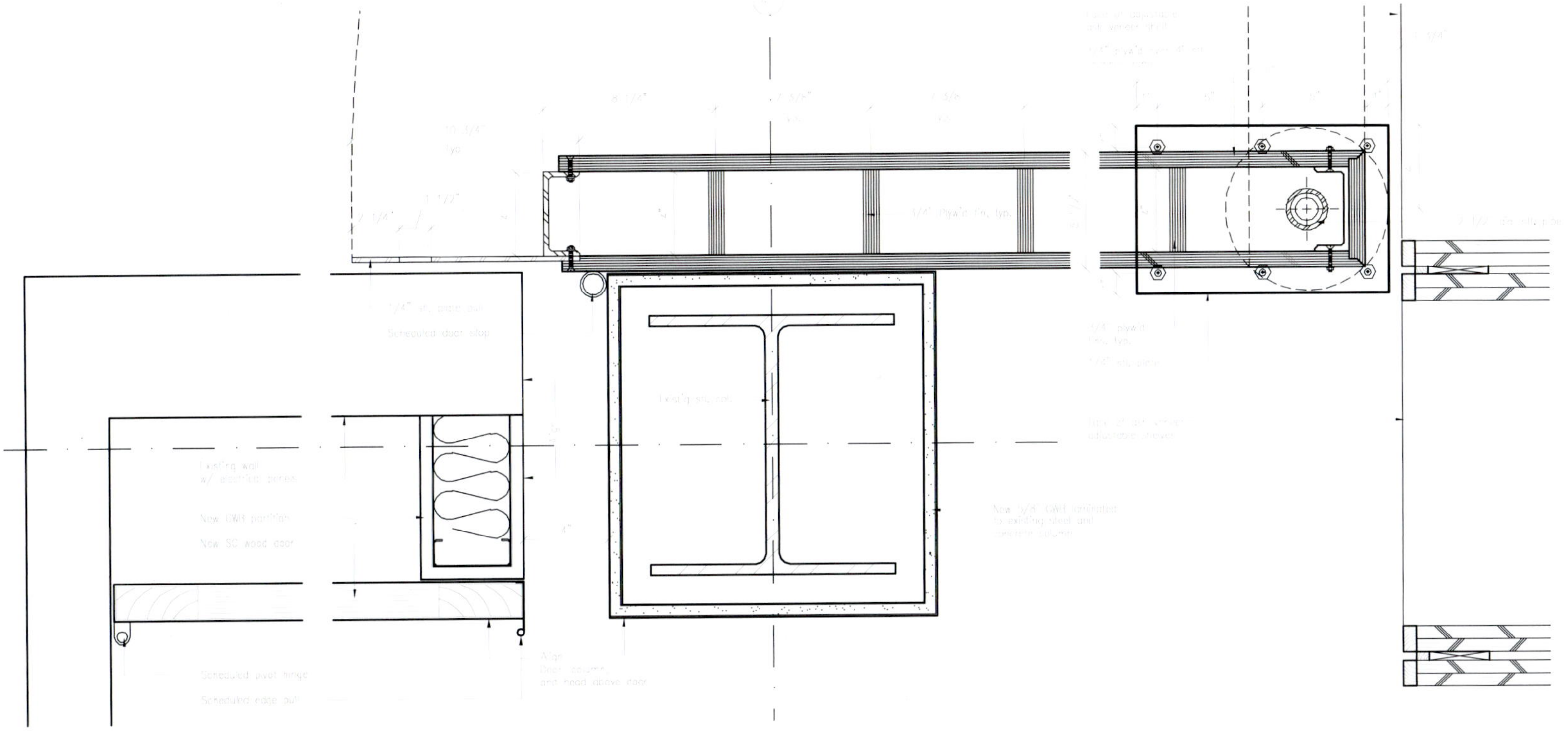

18 PLAN DETAIL @ JAMB, DOOR 144
3"= 1'-0"

17 PLAN DETAIL @ PIVOT, DOOR 144
3"= 1'-0"

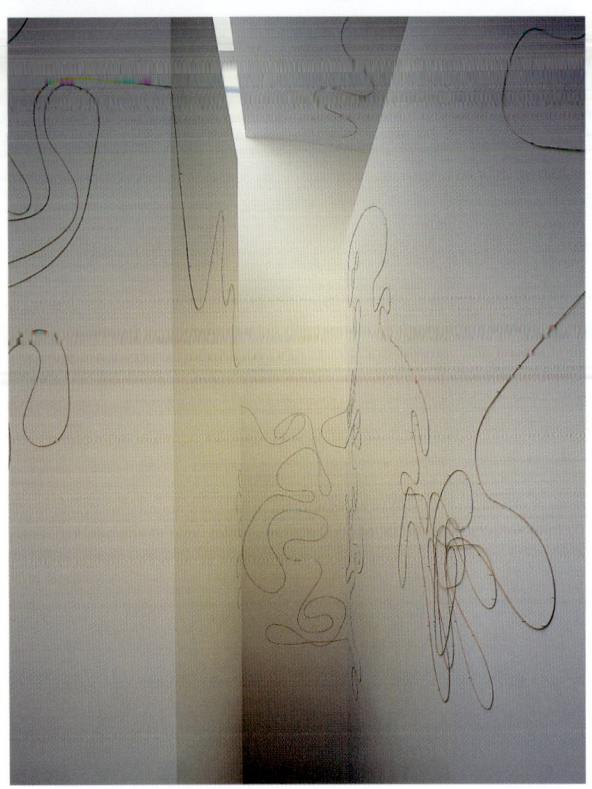

Olson Sundberg Kundig Allen Architects, Garden House, San Francisco Bay Area, 1998. Eine Installation natürlicher Objekte des Bildhauers Andy Goldsworthy belebt die weißen Wände eines Treppenhauses in diesem privaten Wohnhaus.

Olson Sundberg Kundig Allen Architects, maison de jardin, région de la baie de San Francisco, 1998. Une installation d'objets naturels réalisés par le sculpteur Andy Goldsworthy égaie les murs blancs de la cage d'escalier de cette résidence privée.

Olson Sundberg Kundig Allen Architects, Garden House, San Francisco Bay Area, 1998. Een kunstwerk met natuurlijke objecten van beeldhouwer Andy Goldsworthy verlevendigt de witte muren in een trappenhuis in deze woning.

Office for Metropolitan Architecture / Rem Koolhaas und Architecture Research Office, Prada Store, SoHo, New York, 2001. Die durchscheinende Kunststoffwand wird von hinten durch Fenster und farbige Leuchten illuminiert. Das synthetische Material ist über der Decke gefaltet und bildet eine leuchtende Umhüllung des Raumes.

Office for Metropolitan Architecture/Rem Koolhaas et Architecture Research Office, magasin Prada à SoHo, New York, 2001. Le mur translucide en synthétique est illuminé de l'arrière par des fenêtres et des lampes colorées. Sa surface se rejoint au-dessus du plafond pour former une enveloppe brillante entourant l'espace.

Office for Metropolitan Architecture/Rem Koolhaas en Architecture Research Office, Prada Store SoHo, New York, 2001. De doorschijnende synthetische muur wordt van achteren verlicht door ramen en gekleurde lampen. Hij loopt door over het plafond en omvat de ruimte als een gloeiende envelop.

säulen colonnes zuilen

VORHERIGE SEITE: Daniel Rowen Architect, Martha Stewart Living / Omnimedia Offices, New York, 2001. VORLIEGENDE DOPPELSEITE: Davis Brody Bond, Valeo Thermal Systems, Hauptverwaltung für Nordamerika und Technisches Zentrum, Auburn Hills, Michigan, 1998. Ein zugleich einfaches und großartiges System von Sonnenschutzelementen beschattet eine außen stehende Stützenreihe.

PAGE PRÉCÉDENTE : Daniel Rowen Architect, bureaux Martha Stewart Living/Omnimedia, New York, 2001. CETTE DOUBLE PAGE : Davis Brody Bond, Valeo Thermal Systems, siège nord-américain et centre technique, Auburn Hills, Michigan, 1998. À la fois simple et imposant, un système de persiennes abrite une colonnade extérieure.

VORIGE BLADZIJDE: Daniel Rowen Architect, Martha Stewart Living/Omnimedia Offices, New York, 2001. DEZE BLADZIJDEN: Davis Brody Bond, Valeo Thermal Systems, North American Headquarters and Technical Center, Auburn Hills, Michigan, 1998. Eenvoudige doch stijlvolle jaloezieën overschaduwen een buiten geplaatste zuilenrij.

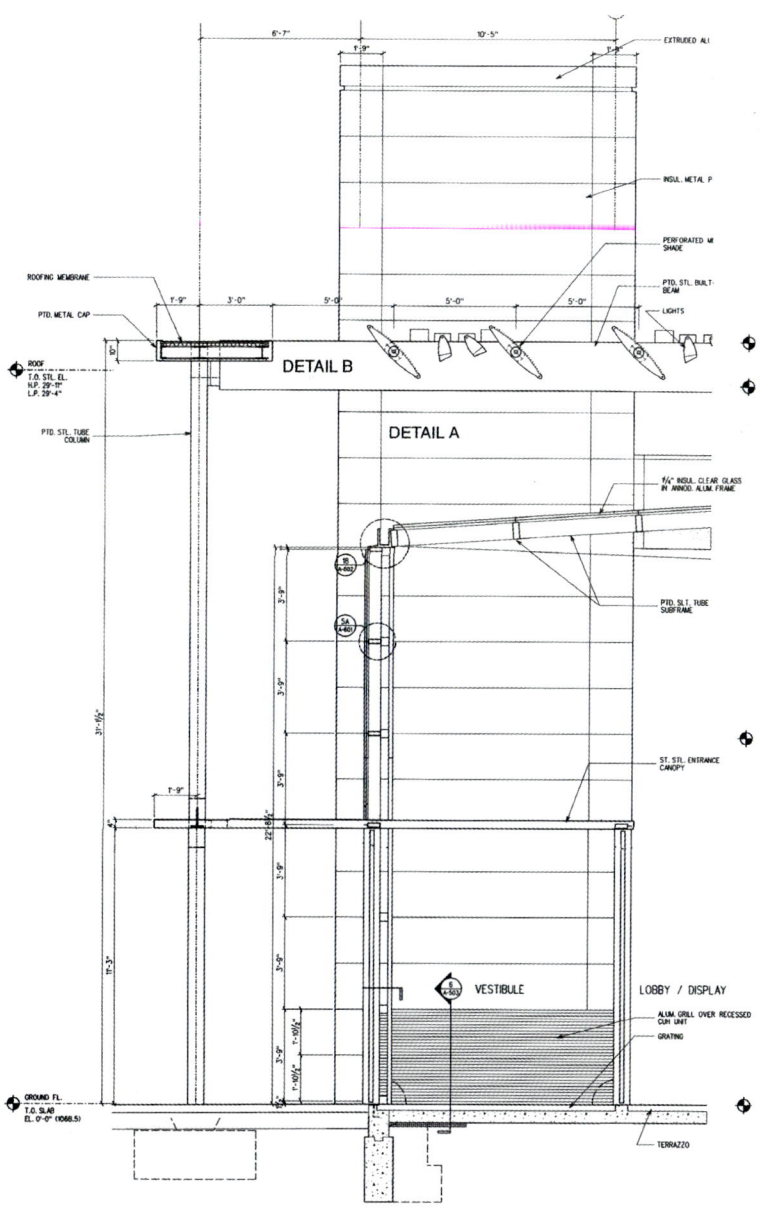

WALL SECTION @ LOBBY ENTRY
SCALE 3/32" = 1'-0"

VORHERIGE DOPPELSEITE: Smith-Miller + Hawkinson, Architects, North Carolina Museum of Arts, Raleigh, North Carolina, 1997. Die schragen Stutzen dieses Amphitheaters und Freilichtkinos sind in unerschiedlichen Winkeln aufgestellt. VORLIEGENDE DOPPELSEITE: Steven Holl Architects, Y House, nördlich von New York, 1999. Eine Interpretation des 21. Jahrhunderts der traditionellen Wohnhauselemente Veranda und Balkon mit Ausblick auf die Catskill Mountains.

DOUBLE PAGE PRÉCÉDENTE : Smith-Miller + Hawkinson Architects, Musée d'art de la Caroline du Nord, Raleigh, Caroline du Nord, 1997. Un amphithéâtre et un cinéma en plein air se distinguent par des colonnes se dressant à angles variés. CETTE DOUBLE PAGE : Steven Holl Architects, maison en Y, Upstate New York, 1999. Une interprétation du XXIe siècle du porche et du balcon traditionnels surplombe les montagnes Catskill.

VORIGE BLADZIJDEN: Smith-Miller + Hawkinson Architects, North Carolina Museum of Art, Raleigh, North Carolina, 1997. Dit amfitheater annex openluchtbioscoop heeft onder diverse hoeken naar buiten staande zuilen. DEZE BLADZIJDEN: Steven Holl Architects, Y House, Upstate New York, 1999. Een 21e-eeuwse interpretatie van een traditionele veranda en een balkon met uitzicht op de Catskill Mountains.

Steven Holl Architects, Texas Stretto House, Dallas, 1992. Dünne Stützen tragen gekrümmte Dachsegmente, die wiederum die verschiedenen Trakte des Hauses unter sich vereinigen.

Steven Holl Architects, maison Stretto, Dallas, Texas, 1992. De fines colonnes soutiennent les sections du toit incurvé, lesquelles à leur tour relient les diverses ailes de la maison.

Steven Holl Architects, Texas Stretto House, Dallas, 1992. Dunne zuilen dragen gebogen dakdelen, die op hun beurt de verschillende vleugels van het huis met elkaar verbinden.

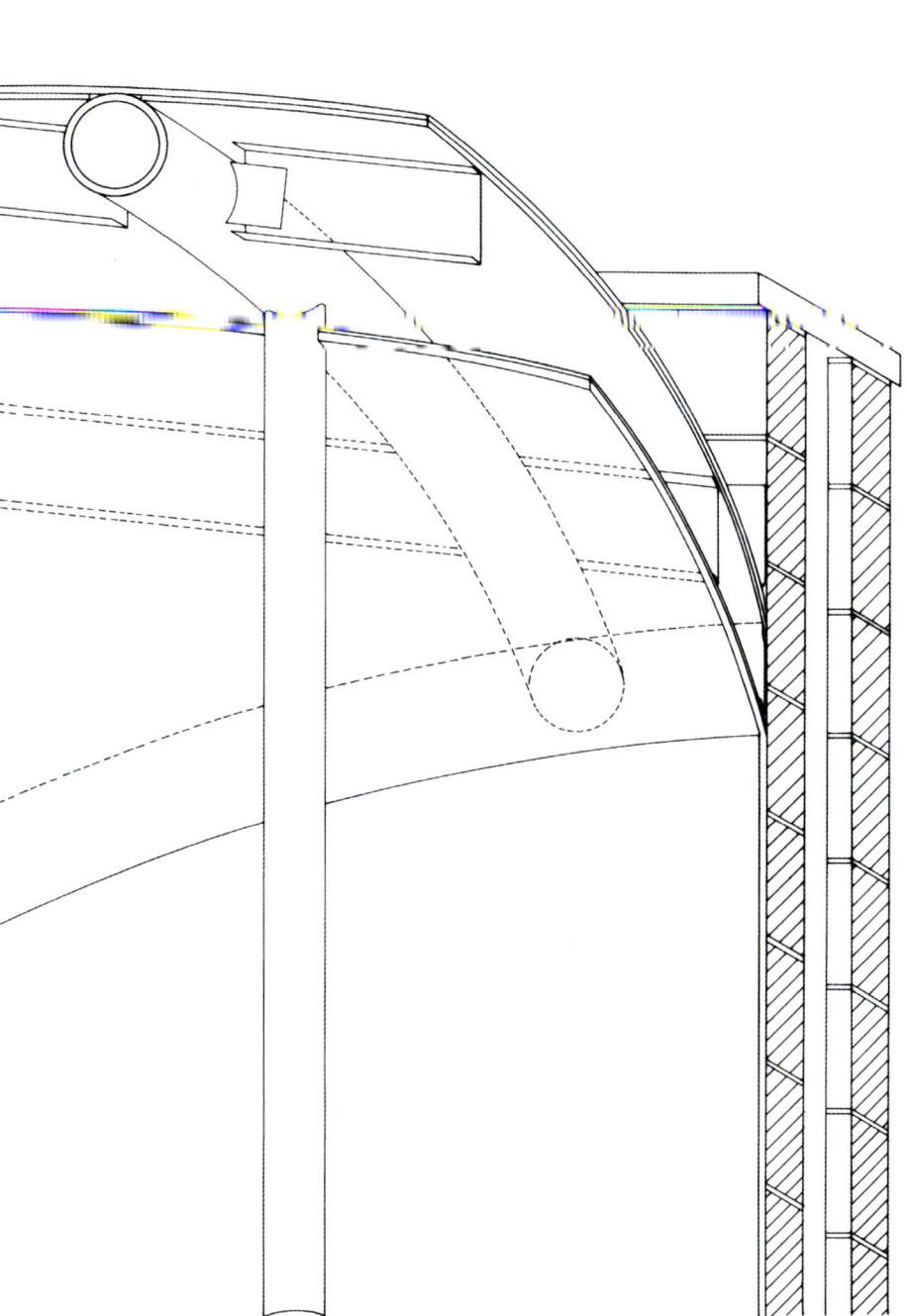

Steven Holl Architects, Wohnanlage Makuhari, Chiba, Japan, 1996. Der Tradition der Moderne folgend, heben die Stützen das ganze Gebäude an und geben den Boden zur Nutzung als Garten und Aufenthaltsbereich frei. Eine Treppe führt von hier in das Zentrum eines Gebäudes mit schrägem Dach, das sich scheinbar zum Himmel reckt.

Steven Holl Architects, logements Makuhari, Chiba, Japon, 1996. Conformément à la tradition moderniste, les colonnes rehaussent l'ensemble de la structure et libèrent la surface au sol en faveur d'espaces verts et d'habitations. Des escaliers mènent d'un jardin au cœur du bâtiment, lui-même semblant s'élever vers le ciel.

Steven Holl Architects, Makuhari Housing, Chiba, Japan, 1996. Conform de modernistische traditie wordt de constructie door zuilen opgetild, waardoor op de grond ruimte ontstaat voor beplanting en bewoning. Trappen leiden naar een tuin binnen in het gebouw, dat naar de hemel lijkt te reiken.

Brian Healy Architects (mit Michael Ryan), Haus am Strand, Loveladies, New Jersey, 1997. Eine Stütze verbreitert sich zu einer hölzernen Bank in diesem Ferienhaus einer Familie an der Küste von New Jersey.

Brian Healy Architects (avec Michael Ryan), maison de plage, Loveladies, New Jersey, 1997. Une colonne se prolonge en un banc de bois devant cette maison de plage familiale, située sur les côtes du New Jersey.

Brian Healy Architects (met Michael Ryan), Beach House, Loveladies, New Jersey, 1997. Een zuil dient tevens als houten bank in dit strandhuis aan de kust van New Jersey.

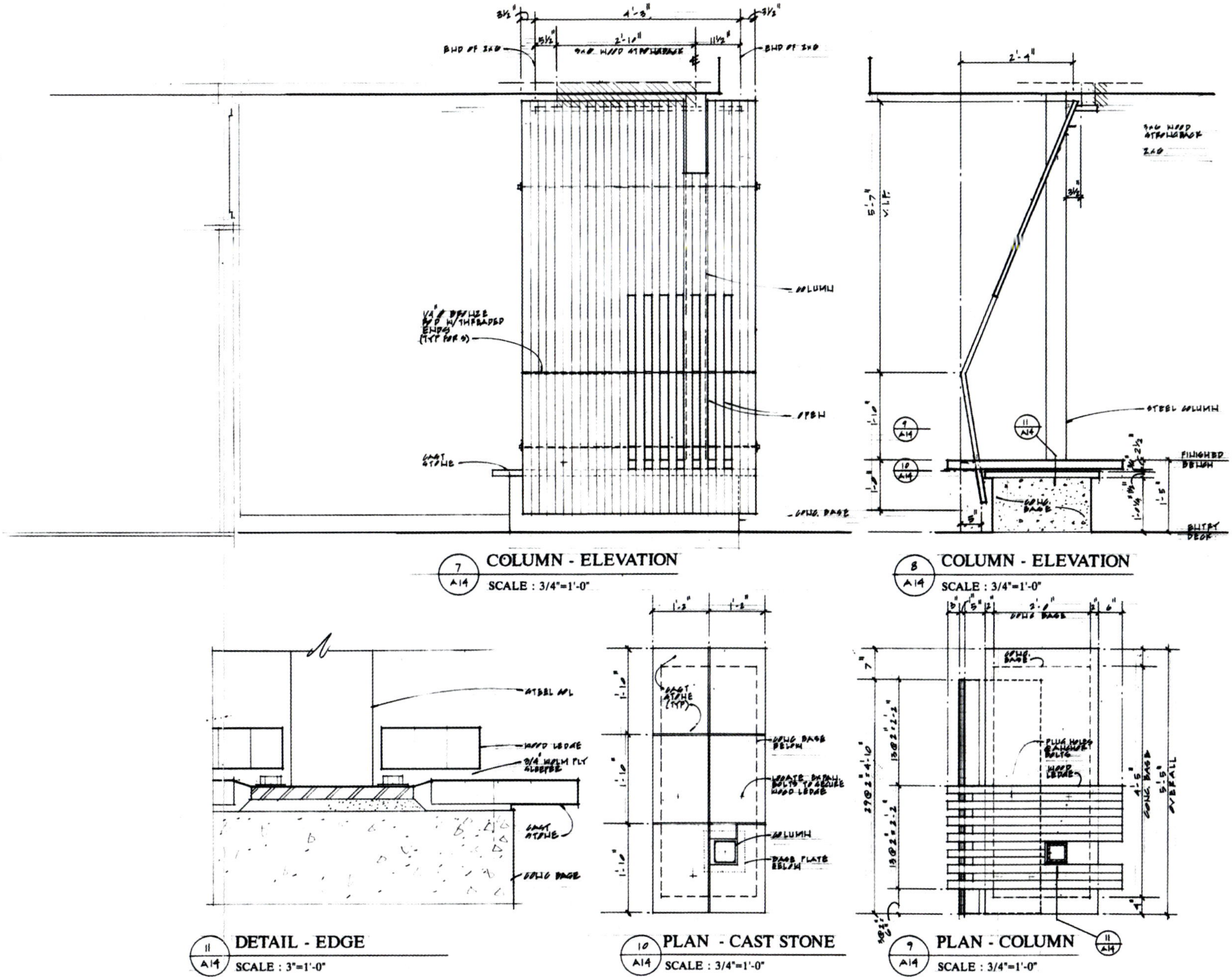

7 — COLUMN - ELEVATION SCALE : 3/4"=1'-0"

8 — COLUMN - ELEVATION SCALE : 3/4"=1'-0"

11 — DETAIL - EDGE SCALE : 3"=1'-0"

10 — PLAN - CAST STONE SCALE : 3/4"=1'-0"

9 — PLAN - COLUMN SCALE : 3/4"=1'-0"

Maria Hellerstein und Nikolai Katz von HellKatz Architecture and Design, Starret LeHigh Building, New York, 2000. Die frei geformten Kapitelle in der Lobby dieses Bürohauses sind handgefertigt aus Gips, einer Calla-Blüte nachgebildet.

Maria Hellerstein and Nikolai Katz of HellKatz Architecture and Design, Starret LeHigh Building, New York, 2000. Dans le hall de cet immeuble de bureaux, les chapiteaux à forme libre sont en plâtre travaillé à la main et s'inspirent de la forme du lys calla.

Maria Hellerstein en Nikolai Katz van HellKatz Architecture and Design, Starret LeHigh Building, New York, 2000. De kapitelen in de hal van dit kantoorgebouw zijn met de hand gemodelleerd naar de vorm van een witte aronskelk.

Deborah Berke & Partners, Wohnung Howell (Loft), New York, 1999. Als Wohnraum, der sich zur Galerie erweitert, hat dieser Wohn-/Arbeitsbereich Säulen mit konischen Abschlüssen.

Deborah Berke & Partners, loft Howell, New York, 1999. Loft résidentiel faisant également office de galerie, cet espace de vie et de travail se distingue par des colonnes évasées.

Deborah Berke & Partners, Howell Loft, New York, 1999. Deze loft, die tevens als galerie dient, heeft in de woon- en werk-ruimte zuilen met uitlopende bovenkanten.

Daniel Rowen Architect, Martha Stewart Living/Omnimedia Offices, New York, 2001. Eine prächtige doppelte Kolonnade begrenzt diesen weitläufigen, sonnendurchfluteten Arbeitsbereich.

Daniel Rowen Architect, bureaux Martha Stewart Living/Omnimedia, New York, 2001. Une double colonnade seigneuriale définit cet endroit de travail étendu et baigné par le soleil.

Daniel Rowen Architect, Martha Stewart Living/Omnimedia Offices, New York, 2001. Deze ruime, zonovergoten werkruimte wordt gekenmerkt door een statige dubbele zuilenrij.

oberlichter lucarnes dakramen

VORHERIGE SEITE: Steven Holl Architects, Kapelle St. Ignatius, Seattle, 1997. VORLIEGENDE DOPPELSEITE: Museum für zeitgenössische Kunst, Helsinki, 1998. Die „erkerförmigen" Oberlichter scheinen sich aus dem gekrümmten Metalldach zu schälen und lassen gefiltertes Licht in die Ausstellungsräume.

PAGE PRÉCÉDENTE : Steven Holl Architects, chapelle St. Ignatius, Seattle, 1997. CETTE DOUBLE PAGE : Steven Holl Architects, Musée d'art contemporain, Helsinki, 1998. Les lucarnes « nœud papillon » de l'architecte semblent se détacher du toit métallique incurvé, laissant la lumière naturelle pénétrer dans les galeries du musée.

VORIGE BLADZIJDE: Steven Holl Architects, Chapel of St. Ignatius, Seattle, 1997. DEZE BLADZIJDEN: Steven Holl Architects, Museum of Contemporary Art, Helsinki, 1998. Deze 'vlinderdasvormige'-dakramen lijken uit de welving van het metalen dak te steken, waardoor daglicht kan doordringen tot de galerieën van het museum.

VORHERIGE DOPPELSEITE: Steven Holl Architects, Kapelle St. Ignatius, Seattle, 1997. Der sakrale Raum ist als eine Folge lichtdurchfluteter Volumen konzipiert. An der Stelle, wo sich diese Volumen treffen, befinden sich Oberlichter in verschiedenen Formen, durch die ein zugleich vertrauliches und geheimnisvolles Licht einfällt. VORLIEGENDE DOPPELSEITE: Steven Holl Architects, Kapelle St. Ignatius, Seattle, 1997. Der Innenbereich der Kapelle ist in farbiges Licht getaucht, obgleich von hier aus nur die reflektierte Farbe und nicht die Oberlichter selbst sichtbar sind.

DOUBLE PAGE PRÉCÉDENTE : Steven Holl Architects, chapelle St. Ignatius, Seattle, 1997. Le lieu sacré est conçu comme une série de volumes remplis de lumière, et là où les volumes se rejoignent, des lucarnes de formes variées répandent de la lumière à la fois intime et mystérieuse. CETTE DOUBLE PAGE : Steven Holl Architects, chapelle St. Ignatius, Seattle, 1997. Les volumes intérieurs de la chapelle sont baignés de lumière colorée, bien que seule la couleur réfléchie et non la lucarne elle-même puisse être vue de l'intérieur.

VORIGE BLADZIJDEN: Steven Holl Architects, Chapel of St. Ignatius, Seattle, 1997. De gewijde plaats is uitgewerkt als een reeks ruimten vol licht. Waar de ruimten bij elkaar komen, zijn er dakramen in allerlei vormen die een geruststellend en tevens mysterieus licht doorlaten. DEZE BLADZIJDEN: Steven Holl Architects, Chapel of St. Ignatius, Seattle, 1997. De binnenruimten van de kapel baden in gekleurd licht, hoewel binnen alleen de weerkaatsing van het licht en niet het dakraam zelf te zien is.

Steven Holl Architects, Bellevue Art Museum, Bellevue, Washington, 2001. Nach den Worten des Architekten wurden die Oberlichter getreu dem „dreifachen Organisationsschema dieses Gebäudes" so gestaltet, dass sie „drei verschiedenen Zeit- und Lichtbedingungen: linear, zyklisch und gnostisch" entsprechen. FOLGENDE DOPPELSEITE: Steven Holl Architects, Bürogebäude in der Sarphatistraat, Amsterdam, 2000. Die Innenräume werden durch „phänomenale farbige Bildschirme" belebt. Diese bilden einen räumlichen und wahrnehmbaren Rahmen, in dem sich die Versorgungsleitungen, Beleuchtung und Belüftung befinden.

Steven Holl Architects, Bellevue Art Museum, Bellevue, Washington, 2001. En respectant la « triplitude », thème directeur du bâtiment, les lucarnes sont conçues pour répondre, selon les mots de l'architecte, aux « trois conditions différentes du temps et de la lumière : le linéaire, le cyclique et le gnostique ». DOUBLE PAGE SUIVANTE : Steven Holl Architect, bureaux Sarphatistraat, Amsterdam, 2000. Les espaces intérieurs sont animés par « des écrans phénoménaux de couleur ». Ces écrans forment un cadre spatial et expérimental comprenant les équipements, l'éclairage et des grilles d'aération.

Steven Holl Architects, Bellevue Art Museum, Bellevue, Washington, 2001. Conform het 'drieledige' thema van het gebouw zijn de dakramen zo ontworpen dat ze volgens de architect beantwoorden aan de "drie verschillende condities van tijd en licht: lineair, cyclisch en gnostisch." VOLGENDE BLADZIJDEN: Steven Holl Architects, Kantoorgebouw Sarphatistraat, Amsterdam, 2000. De binnenruimten worden verlevendigd door 'fenomenale kleurschermen'. Ze vormen een ruimtelijke en ervaringsomgeving en bieden plaats aan voorzieningen, verlichting en luchtroosters.

Patkau Architects, Wohnhaus in Vancouver, 2001. Vom Pool an der Westseite fällt reflektiertes und auch künstliches Licht bis tief in den zentralen Bereich des Hauses.

Patkau Architects, maison de Vancouver, Canada, 2001. La piscine située sur le côté ouest de cette résidence privée réfléchit et projette la lumière du jour et la lumière artificielle au cœur de l'espace central de la maison.

Patkau Architects, Vancouver House, Vancouver, Canada, 2001. Het daglicht en kunstlicht dat weerkaatst in het lange, smalle zwembad aan de westzijde van deze woning dringt tot diep in het hart van het huis door.

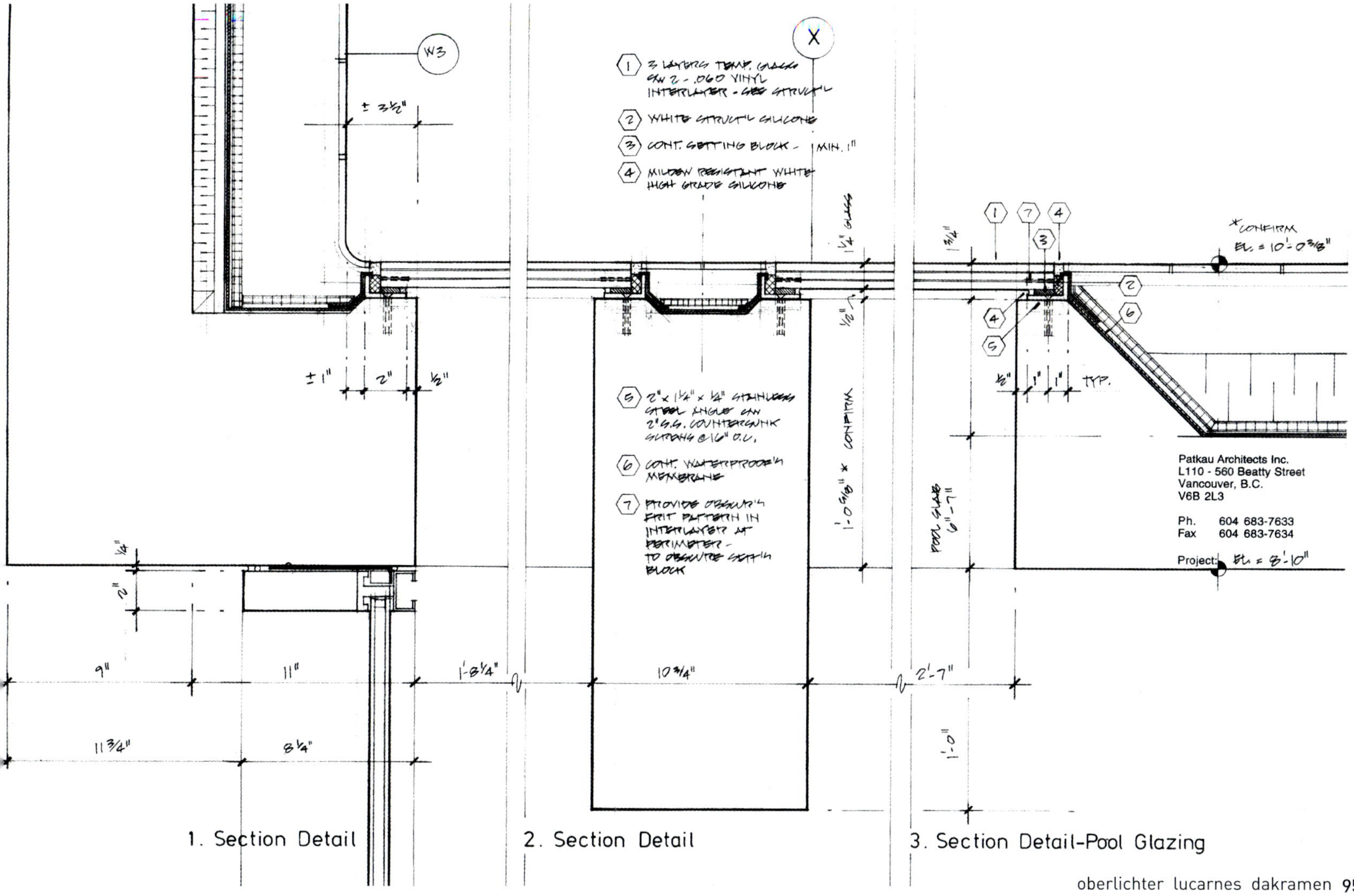

1. 3 LAYERS TEMP. GLASS W/ 2 - .060 VINYL INTERLAYER - SEE STRUCT'L

2. WHITE STRUCT'L SILICONE

3. CONT. SETTING BLOCK - MIN. 1"

4. MILDEW RESISTANT WHITE HIGH GRADE SILICONE

5. 2" x 1½" x ¼" STAINLESS STEEL ANGLE ON 2" S.S. COUNTERSINK BOLTS @ 16" O.C.

6. CONT. WATERPROOF'H MEMBRANE

7. PROVIDE OBSCUR'H FRIT PATTERN IN INTERLAYER AT PERIMETER - TO OBSCURE SETT'H BLOCK

Patkau Architects Inc.
L110 - 560 Beatty Street
Vancouver, B.C.
V6B 2L3

Ph.   604 683-7633
Fax   604 683-7634

Project:

1. Section Detail   2. Section Detail   3. Section Detail-Pool Glazing

Patkau Architects, Wohnhaus in Vancouver, 2001. Diaphane Spiegelungen vom Pool verwandeln eine gewöhnliche Mauer in ein sich ständig wandelndes Wandgemälde aus Licht.

Patkau Architects, maison de Vancouver, Canada, 2001. Les réflexions diaphanes de la piscine transforment un mur ordinaire en une peinture murale de lumière se modifiant constamment.

Patkau Architects, Vancouver House, Vancouver, Canada, 2001. De reflecties van het zwembad vormen op een gewone muur een steeds veranderende muurschildering van licht.

vordächer auvents overkappingen

VORHERIGE, VORLIEGENDE UND FOLGENDE DOPPELSEITE:
Davis Brody Bond, U.S. Bureau of the Census, Administration
and Data Processing Headquarters, Bowie, Maryland, 1998.
Fächerförmig angeordnete, mit Kabeln verbundene Stahl-
streben verleihen diesem Regierungsgebäude ein High-Tech-
Ambiente.

PAGE PRÉCÉDENTE, CETTE DOUBLE PAGE ET LA SUIVANTE :
Davis Brody Bond, Bureau américain de recensement, siège
de l'Administration et du traitement des données, Bowie,
Maryland, 1998. Des fixations d'acier en forme d'aileron et
dotées de câbles prêtent une atmosphère « high-tech » à ce
complexe gouvernemental.

VORIGE, DEZE EN VOLGENDE BLADZIJDEN: Davis Brody, U.S.
Bureau of the Census, Administration and Data Processing
Headquarters, Bowie, Maryland, 1998. Vinvormige, stalen
haken mel kabels geven dit overhcidsgebouw een hightech-
uitstraling.

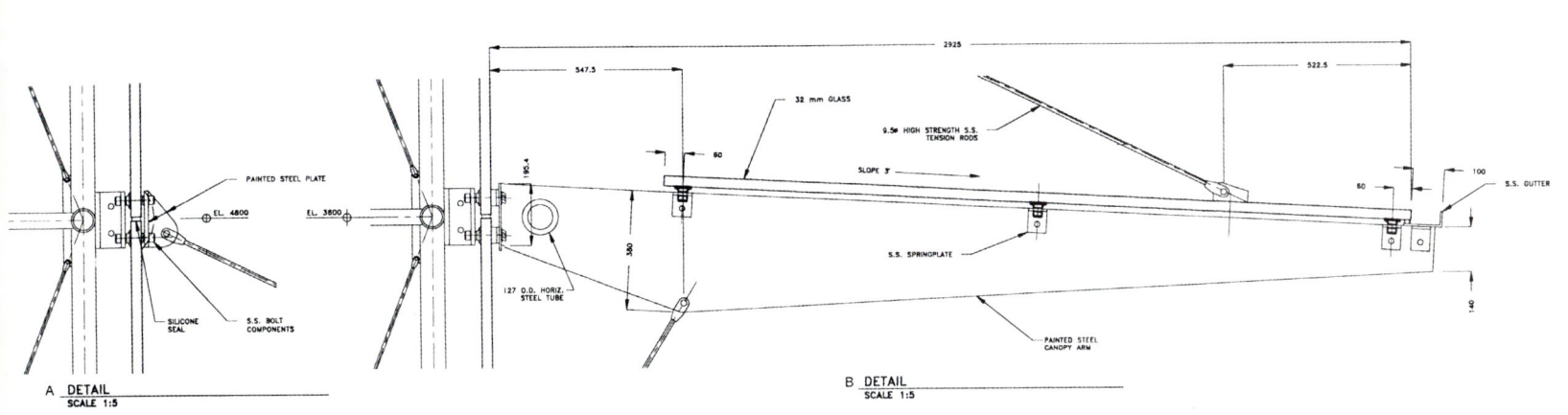

Steven Holl Architects, Cranbrook Institute of Science, Bloomfield Hills, Michigan, 1999. Ein genietetes Vordach aus Stahl markiert den Eingang zur Lobby des Erweiterungsbaus, der ein „Lichtlaboratorium" mit einer nach Süden orientierten Wand aus verschiedenen Glastypen bildet.

Steven Holl Architects, Institut des sciences de Cranbrook, Bloomfield Hills, Michigan, 1999. Un auvent d'acier riveté définit le nouveau hall d'entrée de l'extension, lequel forme un « Laboratoire de lumière » grâce à son mur orienté vers le sud et construit à l'aide de différents types de verre.

Steven Holl Architects, Cranbrook Institute of Science, Bloomfield Hills, Michigan, 1999. De hal van de ingang van de aanbouw heeft een overkapping van staalplaten met klinknaden, die een 'lichtlaboratorium' vormt met een muur op het zuiden die uit diverse soorten glas bestaat.

Parsons + Fernandez-Casteleiro, Architects, Brooklyn Botanical Gardens, Horticultural Services Building, New York, 1998. Ein Vordach aus verzinktem Stahl mit rechtwinkligen Stützen markiert die Hauptfassade des Gebäudes.

Parsons + Fernandez-Casteleiro, Architects, Jardins botaniques de Brooklyn, bâtiment des Services horticoles, New York, 1998. Un auvent d'acier galvanisé aux supports angulaires définit la façade principale de la structure.

Parsons + Fernandez-Casteleiro, Architects, Brooklyn Botanical Gardens, Horticultural Services Building, 1998. De voorgevel van het bouwwerk wordt gekenmerkt door een overkapping van gegalvaniseerd staal met hoekige steunen.

Olsen Sundberg Kundig Allen Architects, privates Wohnhaus, Seattle, 2002. Eine seitlich angeordnete Drehflügeltür aus schwarzem Stahl führt zu einem innen angebrachten Vordach aus dem gleichen Material, das im Verlauf der Zeit eine warme Patina annimmt.

Olson Sundberg Kundig Allen Architects, résidence privée, Seattle, 2002. Une porte pivotante excentrée d'acier noirci mène vers l'auvent de l'entrée intérieure, du même matériau conçu pour se revêtir d'une patine chaude avec l'âge.

Olson Sundberg Kundig Allen Architects, woning, Seattle, 2002. Een excentrische draaideur van gezwart staal leidt naar een overkapte binneningang van hetzelfde materiaal, die zo ontworpen is dat hij een warm patina krijgt in de loop der tijd.

---

④ **ENTRY PARAPET**
  SCALE: 3" = 1'-0"

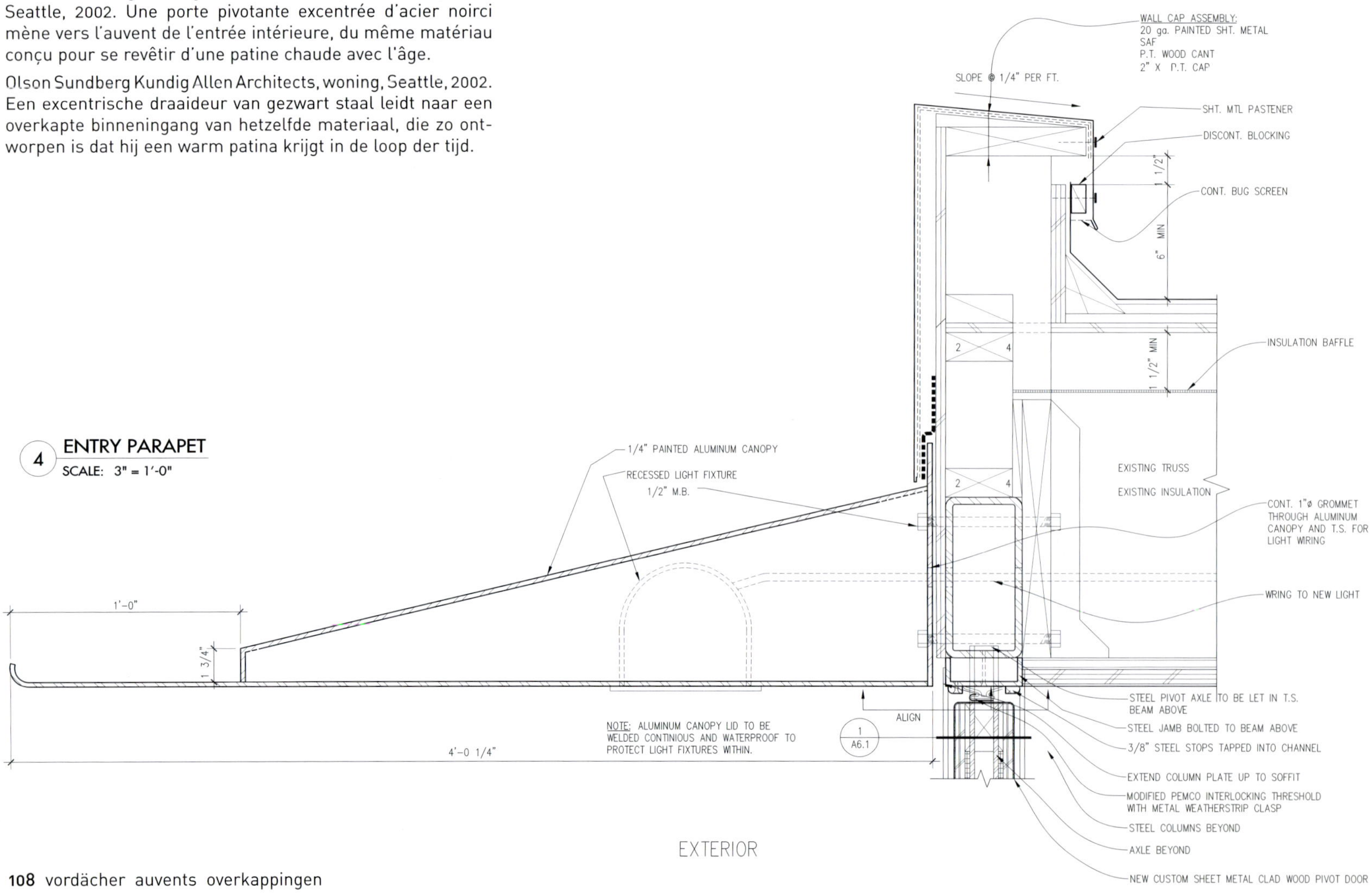

WALL CAP ASSEMBLY:
20 ga. PAINTED SHT. METAL
SAF
P.T. WOOD CANT
2" X P.T. CAP

SLOPE @ 1/4" PER FT.

SHT. MTL PASTENER

DISCONT. BLOCKING

CONT. BUG SCREEN

1 1/2"

6" MIN

1/2" MIN

INSULATION BAFFLE

EXISTING TRUSS

EXISTING INSULATION

2   4

CONT. 1"ø GROMMET
THROUGH ALUMINUM
CANOPY AND T.S. FOR
LIGHT WIRING

1/4" PAINTED ALUMINUM CANOPY

RECESSED LIGHT FIXTURE
1/2" M.B.

2   4

WRING TO NEW LIGHT

1'-0"

1 3/4"

STEEL PIVOT AXLE ITO BE LET IN T.S.
BEAM ABOVE

STEEL JAMB BOLTED TO BEAM ABOVE

3/8" STEEL STOPS TAPPED INTO CHANNEL

ALIGN

①
A6.1

4'-0 1/4"

NOTE: ALUMINUM CANOPY LID TO BE
WELDED CONTINIOUS AND WATERPROOF TO
PROTECT LIGHT FIXTURES WITHIN.

EXTEND COLUMN PLATE UP TO SOFFIT

MODIFIED PEMCO INTERLOCKING THRESHOLD
WITH METAL WEATHERSTRIP CLASP

STEEL COLUMNS BEYOND

AXLE BEYOND

NEW CUSTOM SHEET METAL CLAD WOOD PIVOT DOOR

EXTERIOR

treppen escaliers trappen

VORHERIGE SEITE: Architecture Research Office, Colorado House, Telluride, Colorado, 1999. VORLIEGENDE DOPPEL-SEITE: Patkau Architects, Wohnhaus in Vancouver, 2001. Die Stufen der Treppe nehmen teil am geometrischen Spiel der Wände und Fenster des Hauses.

PAGE PRÉCÉDENTE : Architecture Research Office, maison du Colorado, Telluride, Colorado, 1999. CETTE DOUBLE PAGE : Patkau Architects, maison de Vancouver, Vancouver, Canada, 2001. Les marches de l'escalier s'intègrent au jeu géométrique s'exerçant sur les murs et les fenêtres de la maison.

VORIGE BLADZIJDE: Architecture Research Office, Colorado House, Telluride, Colorado, 1999. DEZE BLADZIJDEN: Patkau Architects, Vancouver House, Vancouver, Canada, 2001. De traptreden maken deel uit van het geometrische spel tussen de muren en ramen van het huis.

Olson Sundberg Kundig Allen Architects, Weinkellerei Mission Hill, Westbank, British Columbia, 2001. Die Wendeltreppe, die zum Glockenturm der Kellerei führt, hat einen Mittelpfosten aus Beton, um den die Stufen angeordnet sind. Jede von ihnen ist fast einen halben Zentimeter schmäler als die darunter liegende, so dass sich die Treppe beim Aufsteigen verjüngt.

Olson Sundberg Kundig Allen Architects, vignoble Mission Hill Family Estate, Westbank, Colombie britannique, 2001. L'escalier en colimaçon menant au clocher du chai est composé d'un noyau central en béton autour duquel les marches se déploient. Chaque marche est d'environ un demi-centimètre plus étroite que la précédente, si bien que la spirale se resserre légèrement vers le haut.

Olson Sundberg Kundig Allen Architects, Mission Hill Family Estate Winery, Westbank, British Columbia, 2001. De wenteltrap naar de klokkentoren van de wijnmakerij draait rond een betonnen kern waaromheen de treden zijn gerangschikt. Elke trede is circa 0,5 cm smaller dan die eronder, dus de trap loopt naar boven licht taps toe.

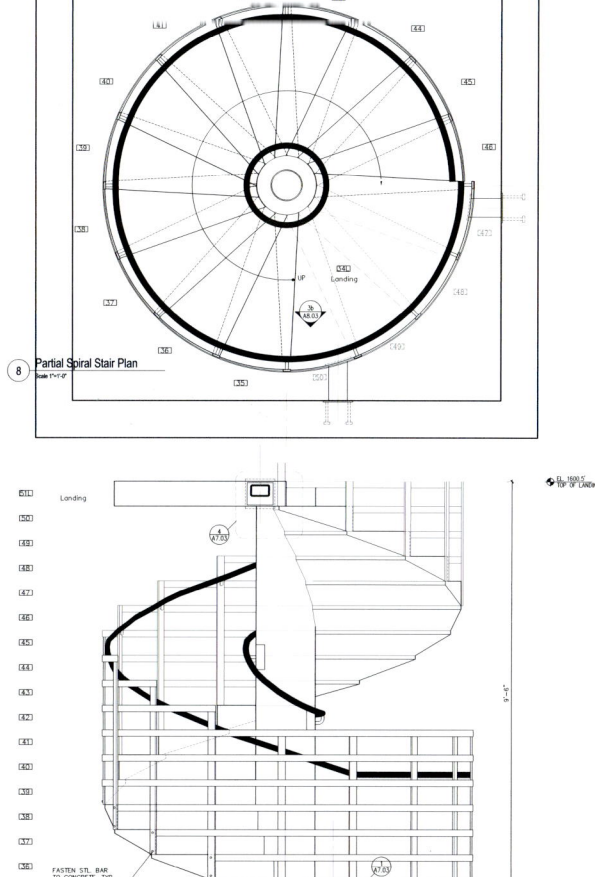

Gabellini Associates, Ausstellungsraum Jil Sander, Mailand, 2000. Eine Treppe ist zum Teil mit fast unwirklich erscheinenden Geländern aus Glas eingefasst. FOLGENDE DOPPELSEITE: Gabellini Associates, Ausstellungsraum Jil Sander, Mailand, 2000. Diese breite, großartige Treppe bildet eine Bühne inmitten des Modegeschäfts.

Gabellini Associates, show-room Jil Sander, Milan, 2000. Un escalier est en partie défini par des rambardes éthérées en verre. DOUBLE PAGE SUIVANTE : Gabellini Associates, show-room Jil Sander, Milan, 2000. Ce large escalier processionnel forme une scène à l'intérieur du show-room de mode.

Gabellini Associates, Jil Sander Showroom, Milaan, 2000. Deze trap wordt deels gekarakteriseerd door een delicate glazen leuning. VOLGENDE BLADZIJDEN: Gabellini Associates, Jil Sander Showroom, Milaan, 2000. Door deze brede, uitspringende trap wordt een verhoging in de modezaak gecreëerd.

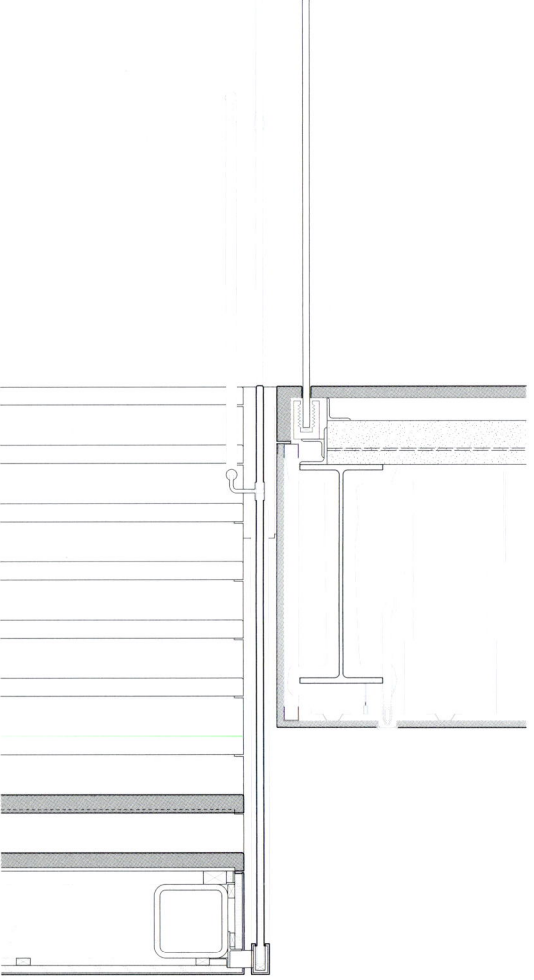

Jay Smith in Zusammenarbeit mit Michael Gabellini von Gabellini Associates, Wohnhaus in der West 12th Street, New York, 1989. Eine weiße Marmortreppe besteht aus einzelnen rechtwinkligen Volumen, die ohne Auflager zu schweben scheinen.

Jay Smith en collaboration avec Michael Gabellini de Gabellini Associates, résidence West 12th Street, New York, 1989. Un escalier de marbre blanc est composé de volumes rectangulaires individuels qui semblent être suspendus sans support.

Jay Smith in samenwerking met Michael Gabellini van Gabellini Associates, West 12th Street Residence, New York, 1989. Een witte marmeren trap met afzonderlijke rechthoekige treden die vrij lijken te zweven.

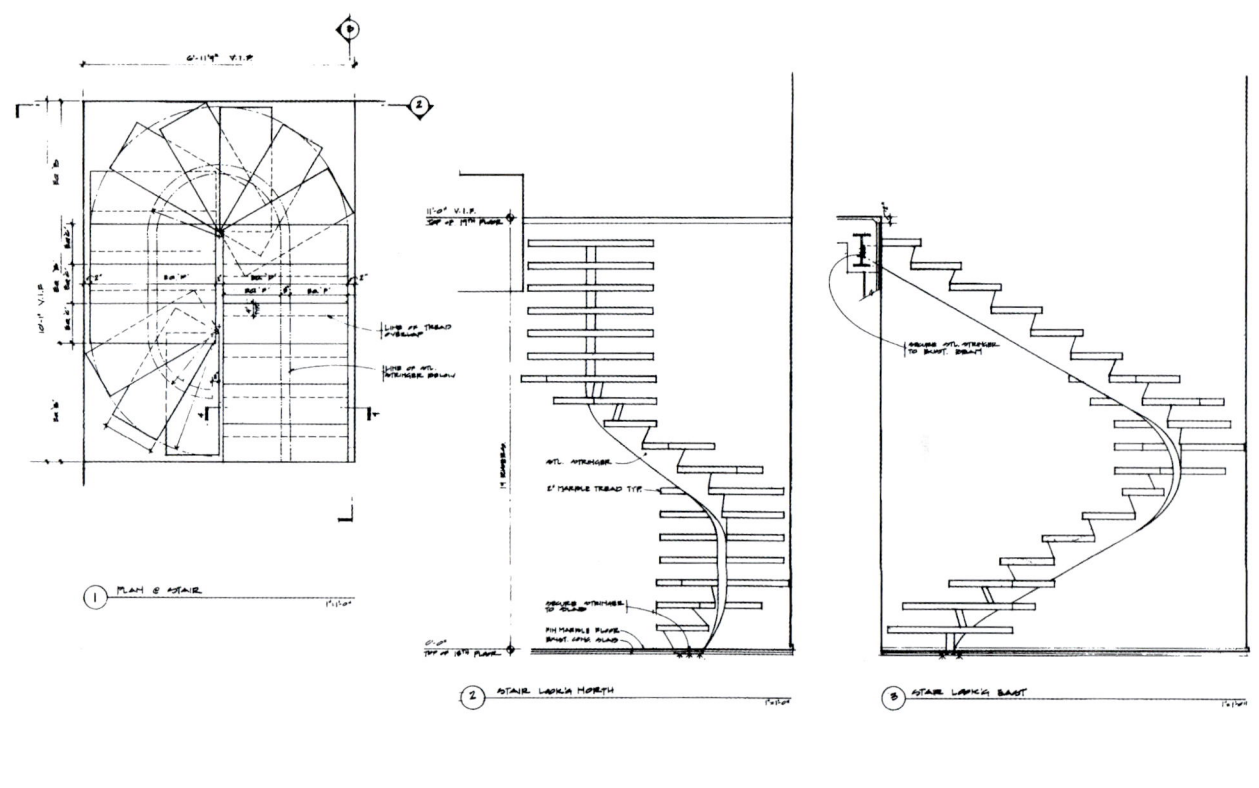

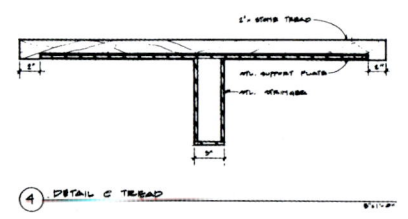

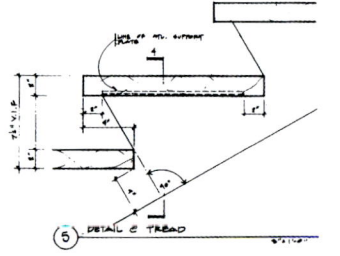

Shelton, Mindel & Associates, Dachwohnung in Manhattan, New York, 1997. Eine gekrümmte Treppe bildet einen starken Gegensatz zu den orthogonalen Trennwänden aus Glas.

Shelton, Mindel & Associates, résidence au dernier étage dans Manhattan, New York, 1997. Des escaliers sinueux et incurvés contrastent fortement avec les cloisons angulaires adjacentes composées d'écrans de verre.

Shelton, Mindel & Association, Manhattan Rooftop Residence, New York, 1997. De curve van de trap vormt een schril contrast met de rechthoekige glazen schermen ernaast.

Architecture Research Office, Loft in Soho, New York, 1999. Die Trittstufen der Treppe wirken wie an den Geländern aus Metall aufgehängt.

Architecture Research Office, loft à Soho, New York, 1999. Les marches de l'escalier du loft semblent être suspendues à des rampes métalliques.

Architecture Research Office, SoHo Loft, New York, 1999. De treden van de trap naar de loft lijken aan de metalen leuning te hangen.

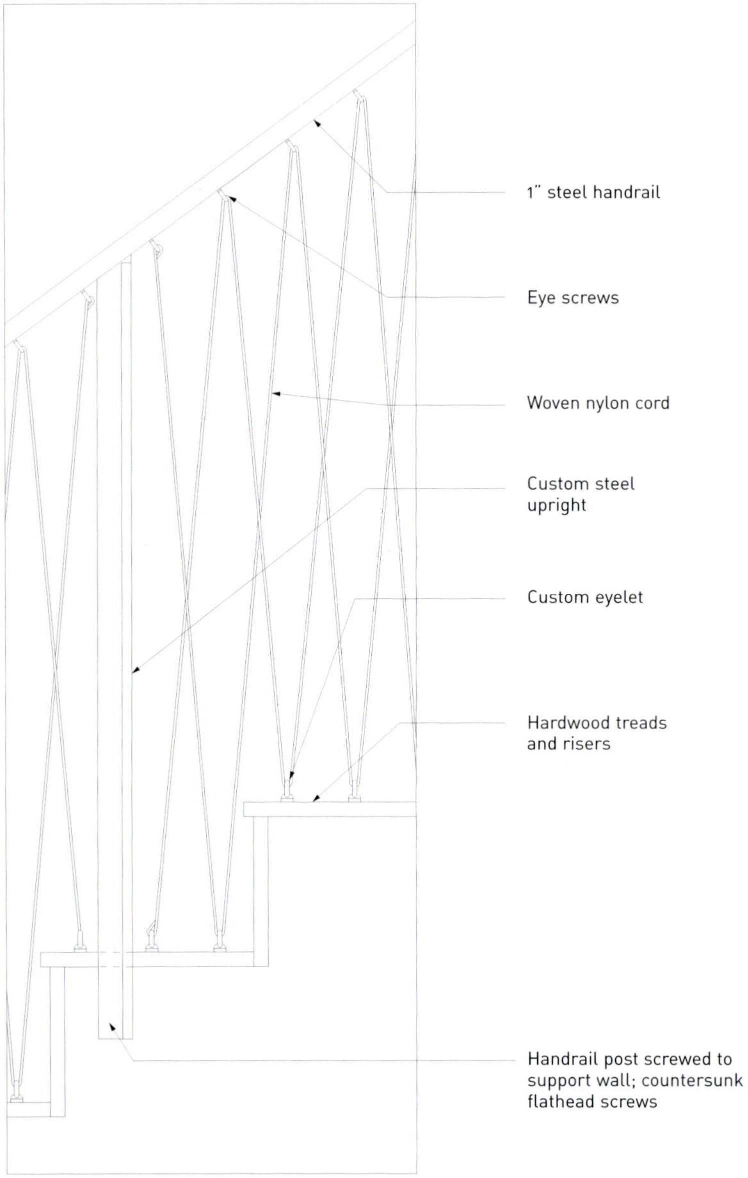

1" steel handrail

Eye screws

Woven nylon cord

Custom steel upright

Custom eyelet

Hardwood treads and risers

Handrail post screwed to support wall; countersunk flathead screws

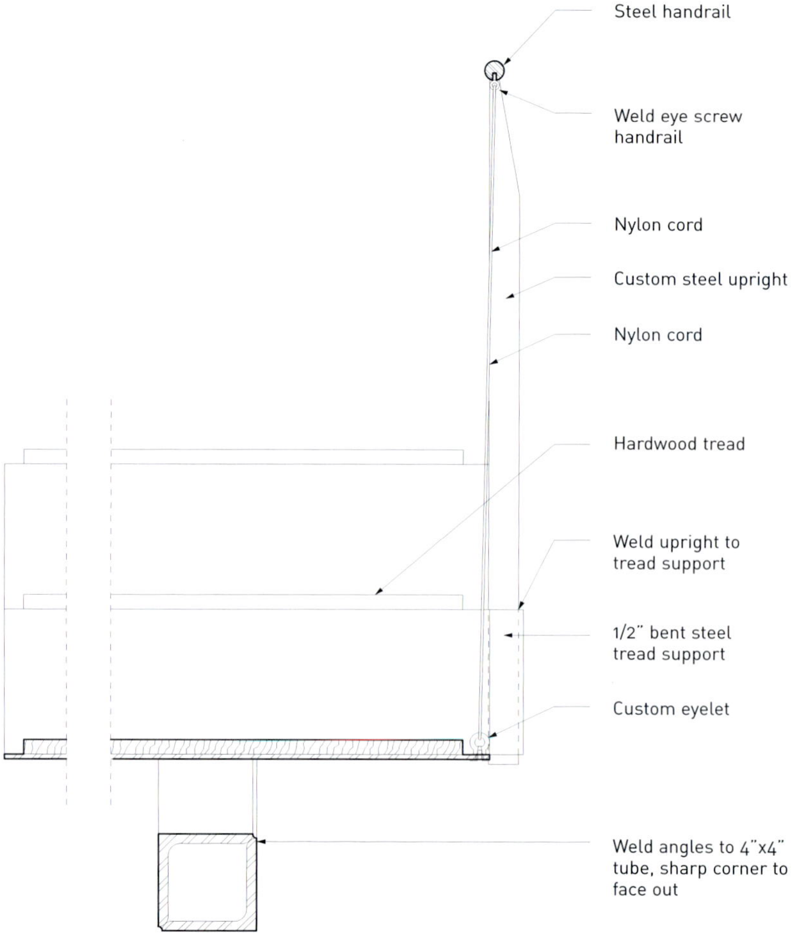

Steel handrail

Weld eye screw handrail

Nylon cord

Custom steel upright

Nylon cord

Hardwood tread

Weld upright to tread support

1/2" bent steel tread support

Custom eyelet

Weld angles to 4"x4" tube, sharp corner to face out

Architecture Research Office, Loft in SoHo, New York, 1999. Eine zweite Treppe in diesem Loft wirkt wie ein an einer Glasscheibe aufgehängter Wasserfall. Ihre Setzstufen aus Stahlrohr sind an Unterstufen aus Walzaluminium befestigt und mit Eichenplatten bedeckt, die als Trittfläche dienen.

Architecture Research Office, loft à Soho, New York, 1999. Un deuxième escalier dans le loft ressemble à une cascade suspendue à une plaque de verre. Ses contremarches tubulaires en acier inoxydable sont reliées par des sous-marches en aluminium laminé recouvertes de plans horizontaux de chêne sur lesquels on marche.

Architecture Research Office, SoHo Loft, New York, 1999. De tweede trap in de loft lijkt een waterval die aan een glasplaat hangt. De stootborden van roestvrijstalen buizen zijn verbonden door ondertreden van gewalst aluminium, belegd met horizontale eiken platen als loopvlakken.

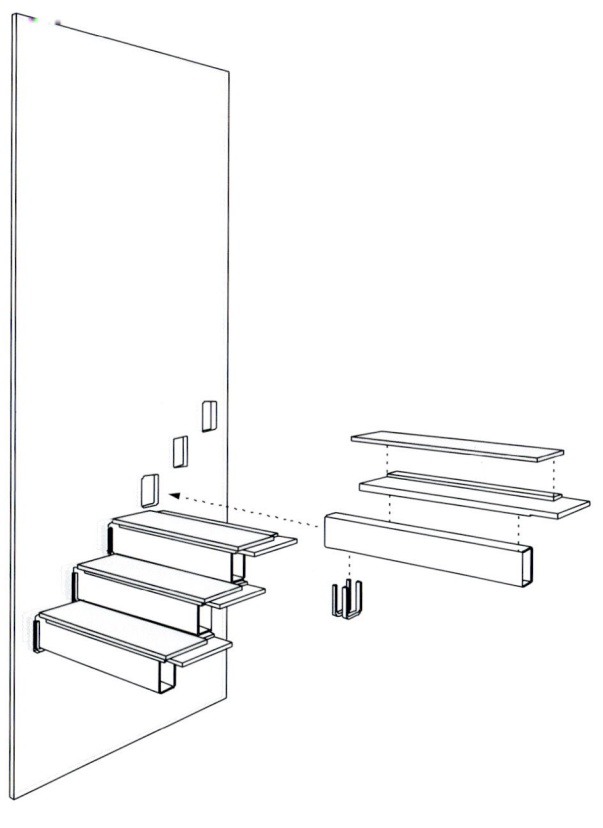

Architecture Research Office, Loft in SoHo, New York, 1999.
Die Architekten behandelten den Punkt, an dem die Konsolen
aus Walzaluminium auf die Verbundglaswand treffen, mit besonderer Sorgfalt.

Architecture Research Office, loft à Soho, New York, 1999. Les
architectes se sont particulièrement appliqués pour l'endroit
où se joignent les fixations en aluminium laminé de l'escalier
et le mur en verre stratifié.

Architecture Research Office, SoHo Loft, New York, 1999. De
architecten besteedden bijzonder veel aandacht aan het punt
waar de gewalste aluminium haken van de trap de gelami-
neerde glaswand raken.

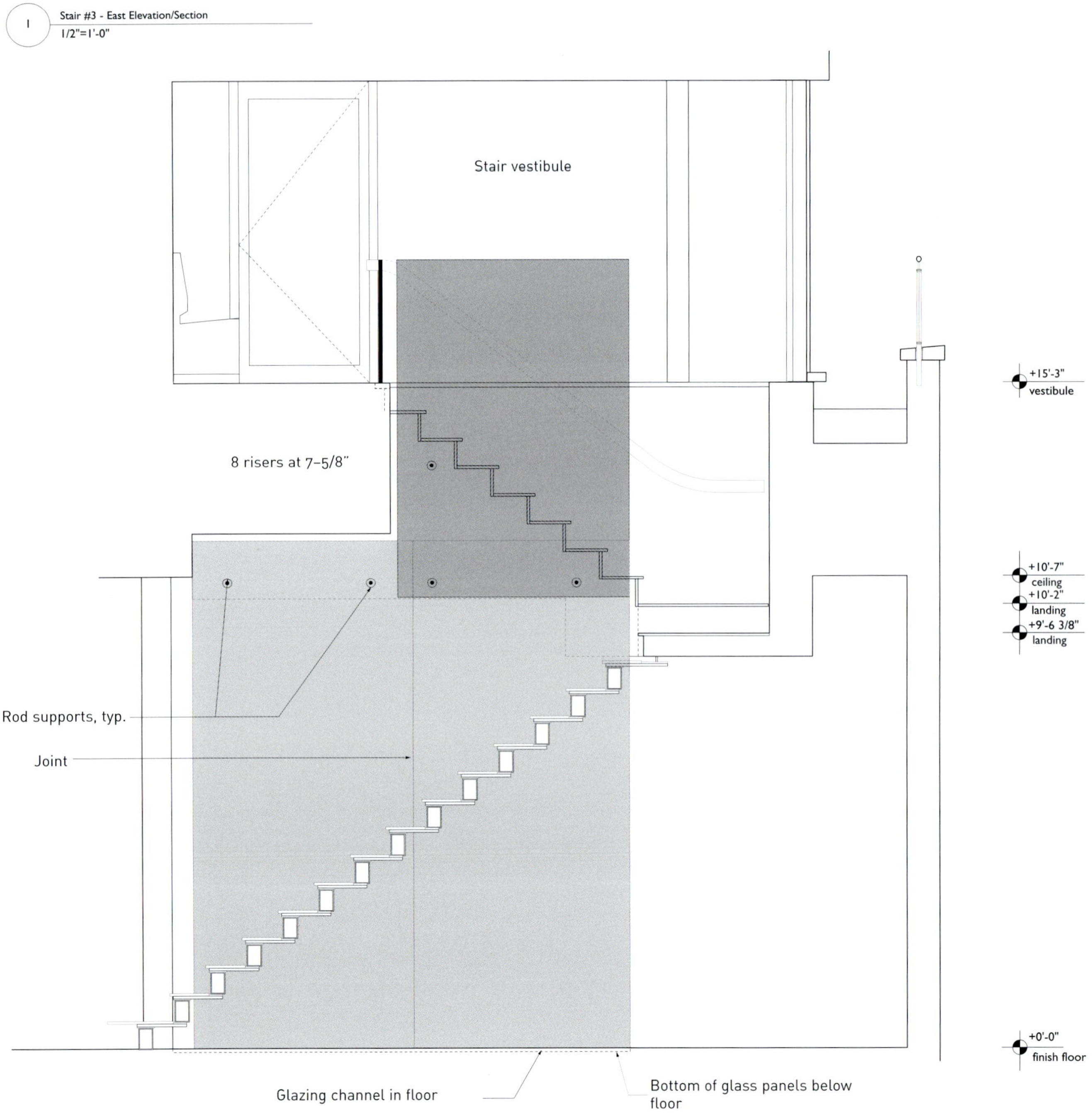

I Stair #3 - East Elevation/Section
1/2"=1'-0"

Stair vestibule

8 risers at 7–5/8"

Rod supports, typ.

Joint

+15'-3"
vestibule

+10'-7"
ceiling
+10'-2"
landing
+9'-6 3/8"
landing

+0'-0"
finish floor

Glazing channel in floor

Bottom of glass panels below
floor

Krueck & Sexton Architects, Stainless Steel Apartment, Chicago, 1994. In einem von Mies van der Rohe geplanten Apartmenthaus machte der Architekt mit einer Treppe aus verwegen auskragenden Stufen aus Edelstahl eine Verbeugung vor dem Meister der Moderne.

Krueck & Sexton Architects, appartement en acier inoxydable, Chicago, 1994. Dans un immeuble résidentiel conçu par Mies van der Rohe, les architectes font un clin d'œil au maître moderniste par le biais d'escaliers d'acier inoxydable audacieusement en porte-à-faux.

Krueck & Sexton Architects, Stainless Steel Apartment, Chicago, 1994. De vrijdragende roestvrijstalen trap in een door Mies van der Rohe ontworpen appartementengebouw was een knipoog van de architecten naar de modernistische meester.

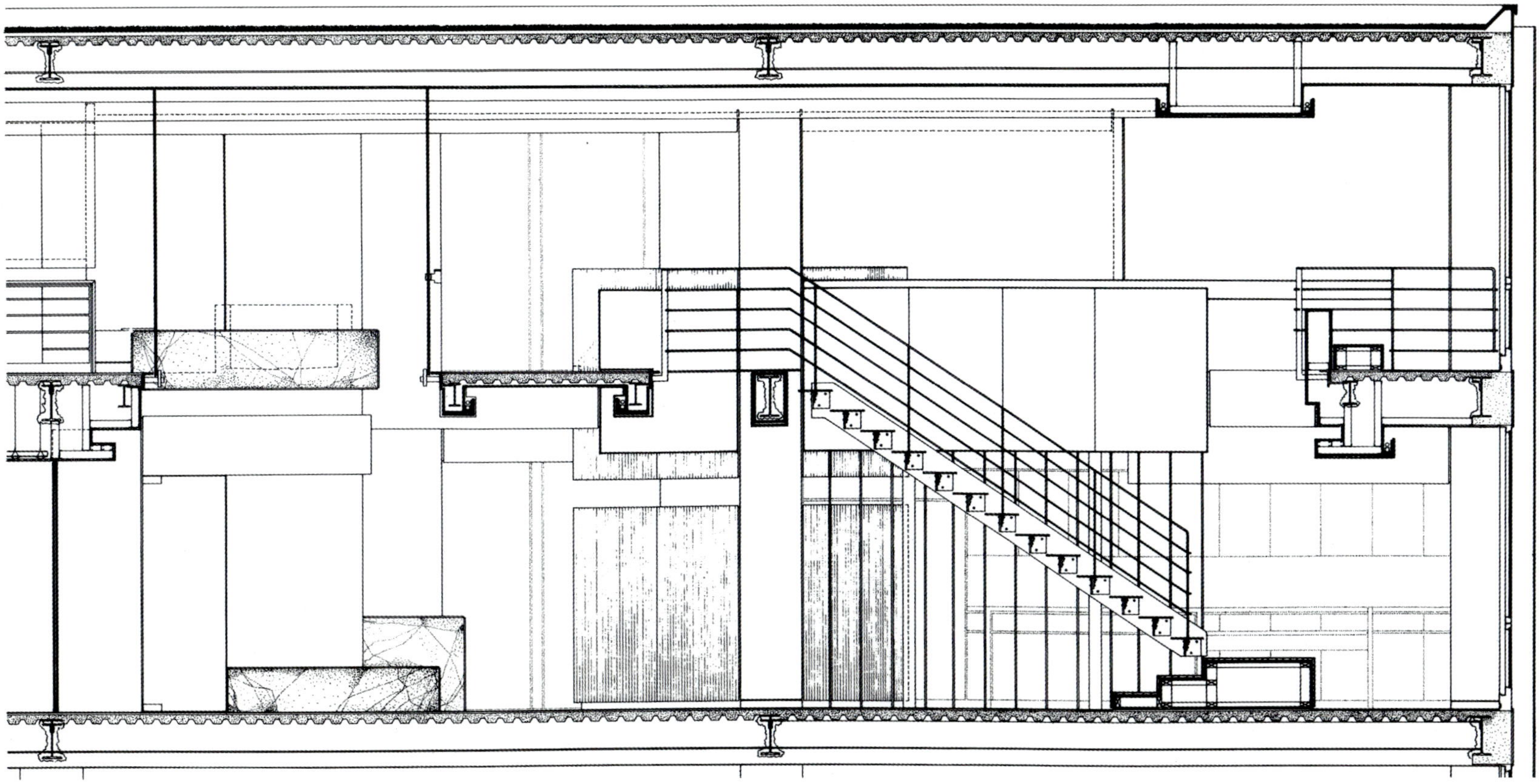

geländer rampes leuningen

VORHERIGE SEITE: Barkow Leibinger Architekten, Customer and Training Center der Firma Trumpf, Farmington, Connecticut, 1999. VORLIEGENDE DOPPELSEITE: Patkau Architects, Wohnhaus in Vancouver, Kanada, 2001. Eine Brücke überquert einen Raum; eine Glasscheibe fungiert sowohl als transparente Wand wie auch als Brüstung.

PAGE PRÉCÉDENTE : Barkow Leibinger Architects, centre de formation et de la clientèle Trumpf, Farmington, Connecticut, 1999. CETTE DOUBLE PAGE : Patkau Architects, maison de Vancouver, Canada, 2001. Un pont traverse l'espace tandis qu'une plaque de verre fait office à la fois de mur transparent et de rambarde.

VORIGE BLADZIJDE: Barkow Leibinger Architects, Trumpf Customer and Training Center, Farmington, Connecticut, 1999. DEZE BLADZIJDEN: Patkau Architects, Vancouver House, Vancouver, Canada, 2001. Een brug doorsnijdt een ruimte; de glasplaat dient als transparante muur en als veiligheidsrail.

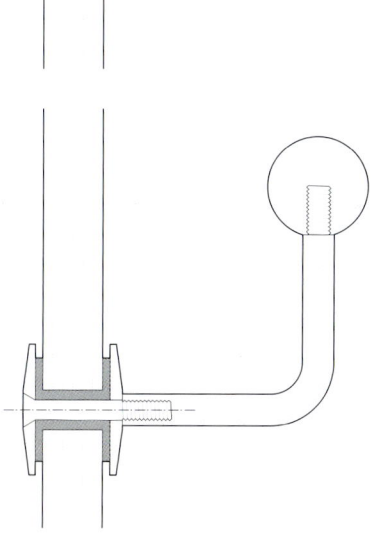

Gabellini Associates, Ausstellungsraum Jil Sander, Mailand, 2000. Der Handlauf aus gebürstetem Edelstahl wirkt schwerelos, als schwebe er auf den strengen Glasflächen, die das Geländer der Treppe bilden.

Gabellini Associates, show-room Jil Sander, Milan, 2000. La main courante en acier inoxydable brossé semble en apesanteur, flottant sur des pans de verre de qualité qui forment la rampe le long des escaliers.

Gabellini Associates, Jil Sander Showroom, Milaan, 2000. De leuning van geborsteld roestvrij staal lijkt gewichtloos te zweven aan de strakke glasplaten langs de trap.

Machado and Silvetti Architects, Büros der Firma Lippincott & Margulies, New York, 1998. Rahmenlose Tafeln aus Milchglas begrenzen das Treppenhaus zwischen oberer und unterer Ebene der Firma.

Machado and Silvetti Associates, bureaux Lippincott & Margulies, New York, 1998. Des panneaux sans cadre en verre laiteux soulignent l'escalier reliant les niveaux supérieur et inférieur de la société.

Machado and Silvetti Associates, Lippincott & Margulies Offices, New York, 1998. Matglazen panelen zonder omlijsting omgeven de trap tussen de verdiepingen in dit kantoorpand.

Architecture Research Office, Loft in SoHo, New York, 1999. Die Tritt- und Setzstufen sind an einem Ende in der Glaswand verankert, am anderen mittels Kabeln am organisch geformten Geländer aus Metall aufgehängt.

Architecture Research Office, loft à Soho, New York, 1999. Les marches et les contremarches sont attachées, à l'une des extrémités, à une paroi de verre, et à l'autre, à des câbles suspendus à la rampe métallique de forme sensuelle.

Architecture Research Office, SoHo Loft, New York, 1999. De treden en stootborden zijn aan één kant verankerd in een glaswand en aan de andere kant met kabels opgehangen aan de aantrekkelijk gevormde metalen leuning.

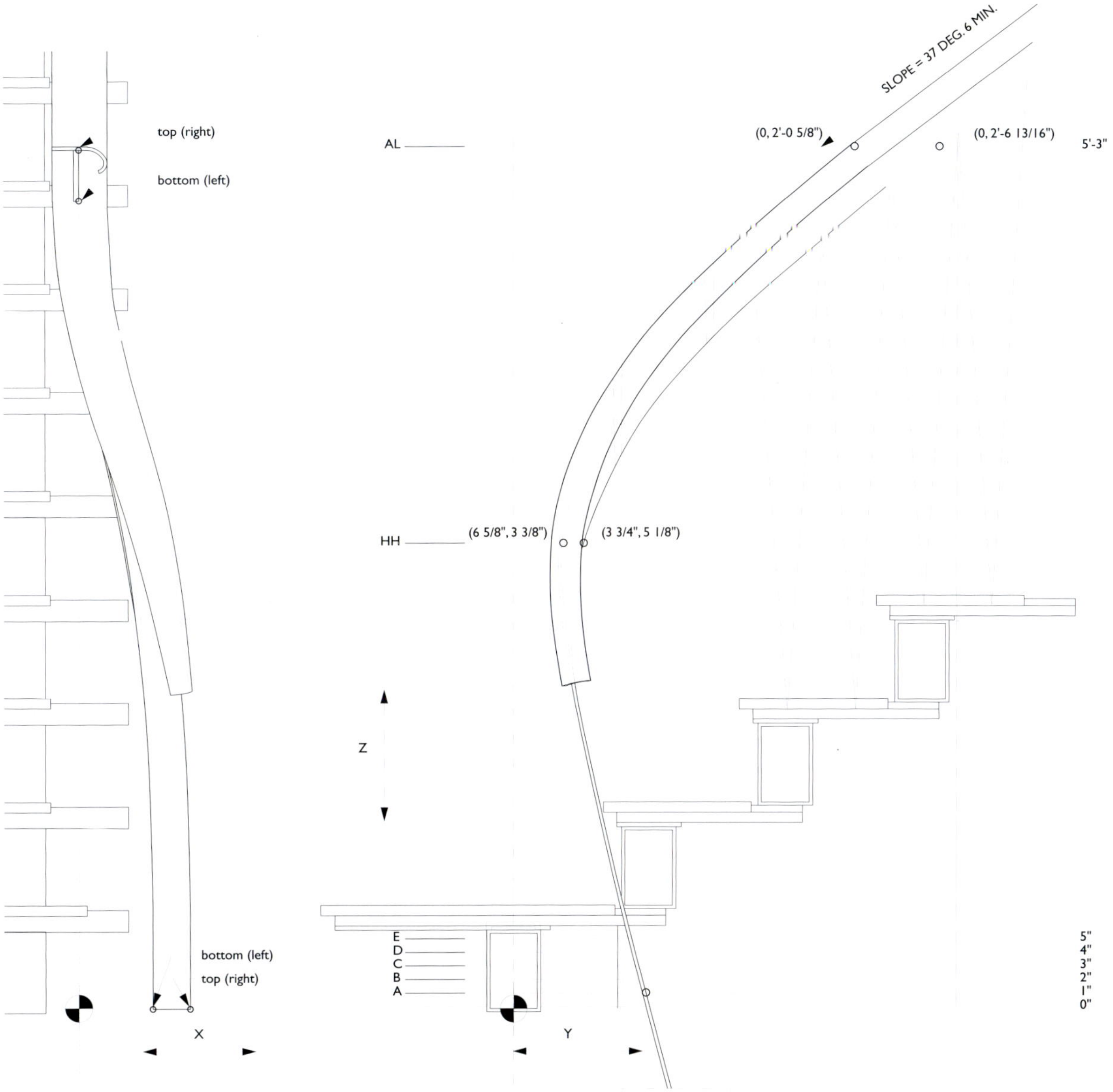

top (right)

bottom (left)

SLOPE = 37 DEG. 6 MIN.

AL

(0, 2'-0 5/8")   (0, 2'-6 13/16")   5'-3"

HH   (6 5/8", 3 3/8")   (3 3/4", 5 1/8")

Z

bottom (left)
top (right)

E
D
C
B
A

5"
4"
3"
2"
1"
0"

X

Y

FRONT   **SIDE**

Hariri & Hariri, Apartment an der Fifth Avenue, New York, 1998. Eine Treppe hat eingespannte Trittstufen ohne Setzstufen und ist optisch zusammengehalten durch ein schlichtes Geländer aus gebürstetem Edelstahl.

Hariri & Hariri, appartement sur Fifth Avenue, New York, 1998. Un escalier est composé de marches en porte-à-faux mais sans contremarches, et il n'est visuellement rattaché qu'à une simple rampe en acier inoxydable brossé.

Hariri & Hariri, Fifth Avenue Apartment, New York, 1998. Een trap met vrijdragende treden zonder stootborden is optisch bevestigd aan een simpele leuning van geborsteld roestvrij staal.

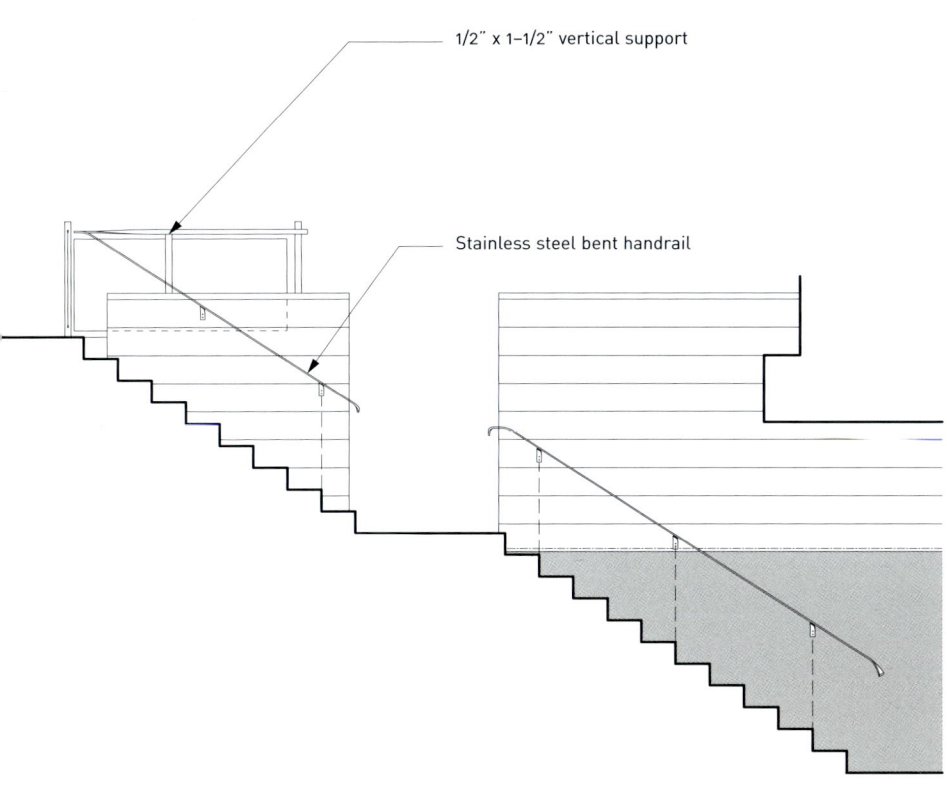

1/2" x 1–1/2" vertical support

Stainless steel bent handrail

Architecture Research Office, Colorado House, Telluride, Colorado, 1999. Ein Geländer verwandelt sich durch eine simple Drehung in einen vertikalen Handlauf. FOLGENDE DOPPEL-SEITE: Maya Lin Studio/David Hotson Architect, Wohnhaus an der Upper East Side, New York, 1999. Eine Einfassung aus schwarzem Stahl bildet das Tragwerk dieser Treppe, das ca. 1 cm starke „Sandwichplatten" aus Holz und schwarzem Stahl trägt.

Architecture Research Office, maison du Colorado, Telluride, Colorado, 1999. Dans un geste élégant, une rampe en inox brossé se transforme en une rambarde verticale grâce à une simple torsion. DOUBLE PAGE SUIVANTE : Maya Lin Studio/ David Hotson Architect, résidence dans Upper East Side, New York, 1999. Un contour d'acier noirci constitue la structure de cet escalier soutené des plaques de bois et d'acier noirci d'environ un centimètre.

Architecture Research Office, Colorado House, Telluride, Colorado, 1999. De leuning van geborsteld roestvrij staal is een elegant en knap staaltje architectuur VOLGENDE BLADZIJDEN: Maya Lin Studio/David Hotson Architect, Upper East Side Residence, New York, 1999. Deze trap bestaat uit verticale stalen stangen die zijn verankerd in de 'sandwiches' van 1 cm dikke houten planken en gezwart staal, waarop de leuning steunt.

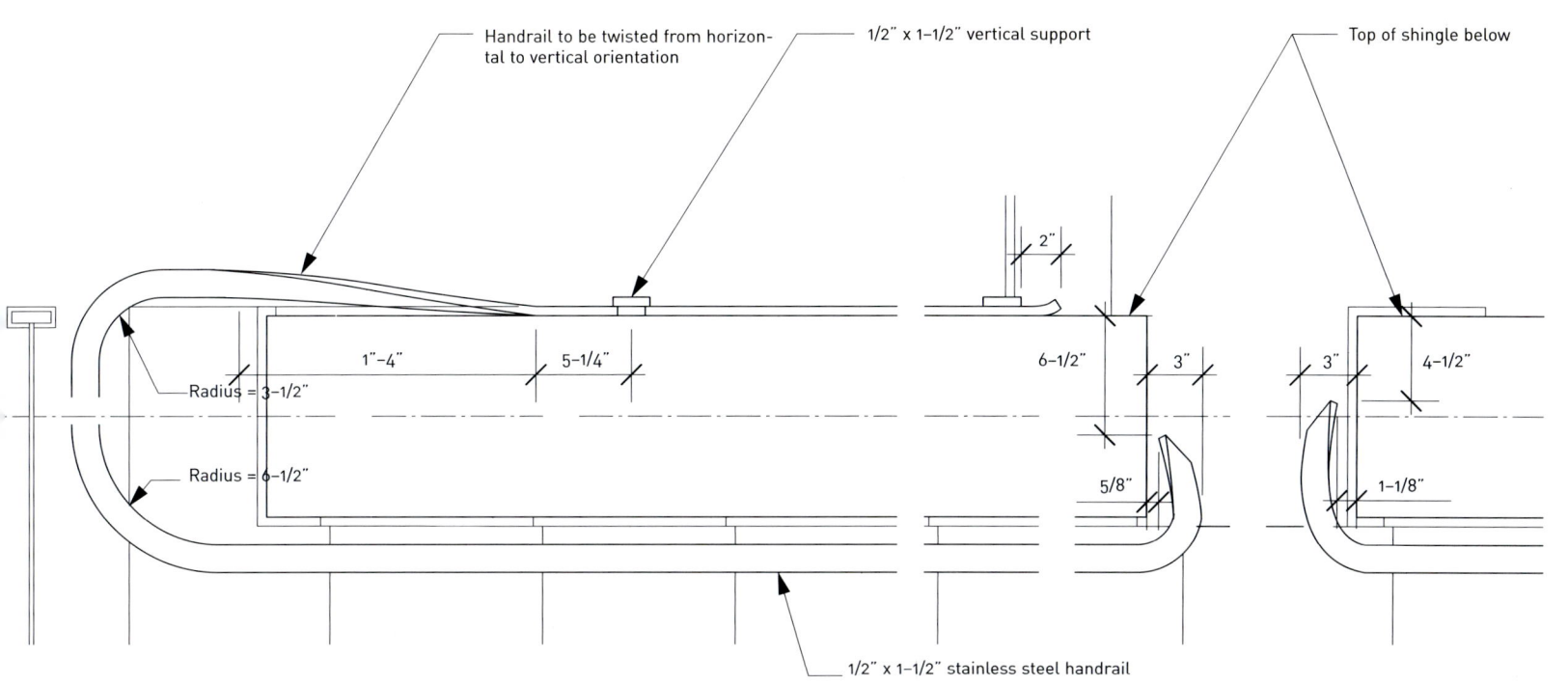

Handrail to be twisted from horizontal to vertical orientation

1/2" x 1–1/2" vertical support

Top of shingle below

2"

1"–4"   5–1/4"

Radius = 3–1/2"

6–1/2"   3"   3"   4–1/2"

Radius = 6–1/2"

5/8"   1–1/8"

1/2" x 1–1/2" stainless steel handrail

Steven Holl Architects, Bellevue Art Museum, Bellevue, Washington, 2001. Das Museum enthält drei Ausstellungsbereiche, die durch eine Treppe mit tiefen Tritt- und flachen Setzstufen verbunden sind. Sie sind zum Teil von gebürsteten Edelstahlgeländern eingefasst. Das Geländer macht am Ende eine geschickte Biegung und wird zum senkrechten Handlauf.

Steven Holl Architects, Bellevue Art Museum, Bellevue, Washington, 2001. Le musée comprend trois lofts en galerie reliés par un escalier aux larges marches et aux contre-marches peu profondes en partie définies par une balustrade en acier inoxydable brossé. La rampe opposée, par le biais d'une adroite torsion, se transforme en support vertical.

Steven Holl Architects, Bellevue Art Museum, Bellevue, Washington, 2001. Het museum heeft drie lofts met galerieën. Ze zijn verbonden door een trap met brede treden en lage stootborden. De leuningen zijn van geborsteld roestvrij staal; de achterste wordt door een handige draai een verticale steun.

Steven Holl Architects, Y House, nördlich von New York, 1999. Wie das Haus selbst, bildet auch die Treppe im Grundriss ein Y. Ihre dunklen Metallgeländer tragen zur Gestaltung der unkonventionell geformten Innenräume bei.

Steven Holl Architects, maison en Y, Upstate New York, 1999. Comme la maison elle-même, les escaliers forment un « Y » sur le plan, et leurs rambardes en métal sombre aident à organiser les espaces intérieurs aux formes non conventionnelles.

Steven Holl Architects, Y House, Upstate New York, 1999. Net als het huis zelf heeft de trap van boven gezien de vorm van een Y. De donkere trapleuningen structureren de onconventioneel gevormde binnenruimten.

Peter L. Gluck and Partners, Architects, Wohnhaus in Highland Park, Illinois, 1998. Der Schnitt in einem gebogenen Aluminiumgeländer zeigt die Form des Fragezeichens, in die es stranggepresst wurde. Die oberen Aluminiumelemente sind mit Brüstungselementen aus Edelstahl verschraubt.

Peter L. Gluck and Partners, Architects, résidence dans Highland Park, Illinois, 1998. La rupture dans la rampe incurvée en aluminium révèle la forme de point d'interrogation à partir de laquelle elle est extrudée. L'élément supérieur en aluminium est fixé aux composants de la rampe en acier inoxydable.

Peter L. Gluck and Partners, Architects, woning in Highland Park, Illinois, 1998. Door de onderbreking in de aluminium leuning is de vraagtekenvorm waarin ze is geperst zichtbaar. Dit aluminium element is vastgeschroefd op roestvrijstalen componenten.

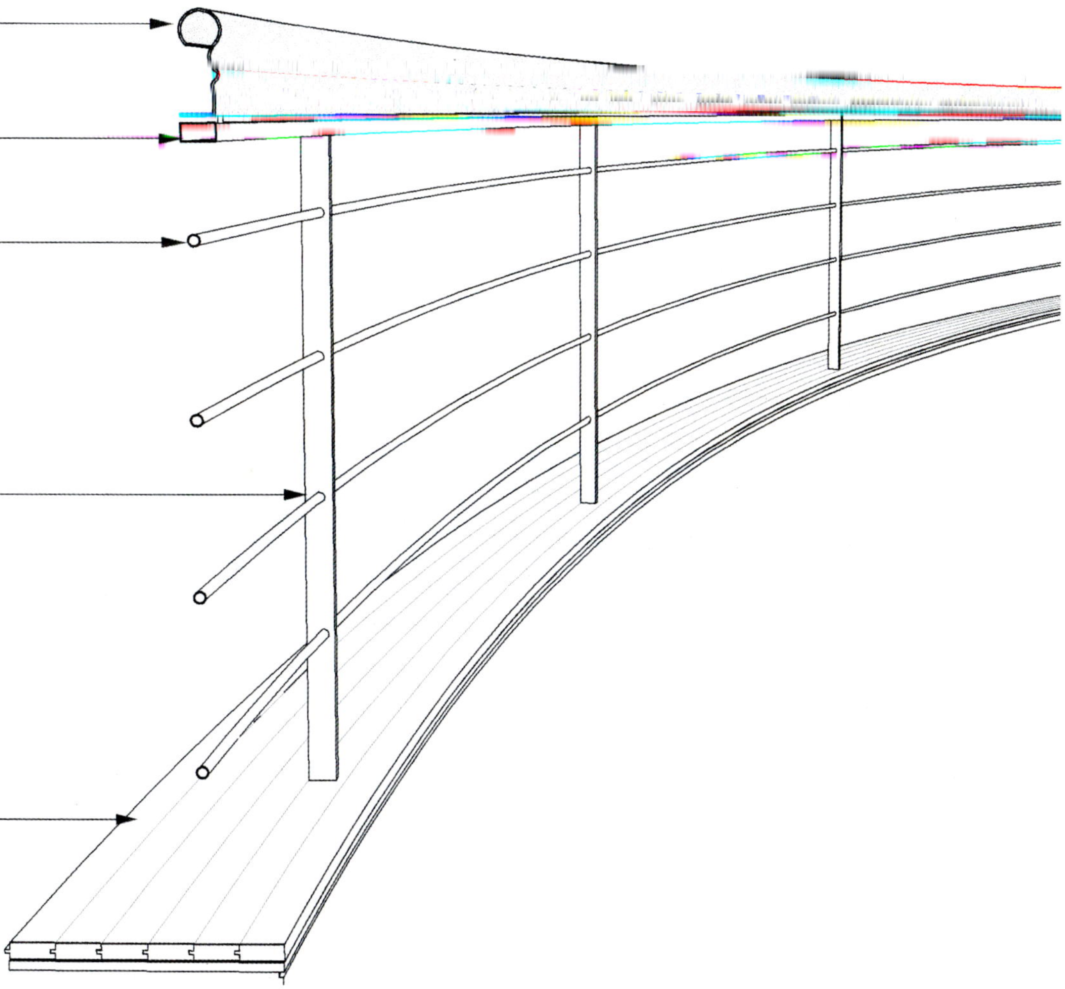

Aluminum extrusion rolled to curve

3/4" x 1-1/2" S.S. bar

1/2" o S.S. rolled to curve

Welded and ground

3/4" x 2" maple flooring

Eric J. Cobb Architect, Haus Cirone Brannon, Seattle, 1999.
Die Teile der Treppe sind als getrennte Elemente behandelt –
ein Geländer aus Metall als Stütze und eine Glasfläche als
Sicherheitsbarriere. Aufgrund ihrer unterschiedlichen Funk-
tion sind die Elemente auch in verschiedene Ebenen gesetzt.

Eric J. Cobb Architect, maison Cirone Brannon, Seattle, 1999.
Les différentes parties de l'escalier sont conçues comme des
éléments séparés : d'une part, la balustrade en métal comme
support, de l'autre, une plaque de verre en tant que barrière
de sécurité. En raison de leurs usages différents, les éléments sont donc fixés sur des surfaces différentes.

Eric J. Cobb Architect, Cirone Brannon House, Seattle, 1999.
De trap bestaat uit afzonderlijke delen: een metalen leuning
als steun en een glasplaat voor de veiligheid. Gezien hun ver-
schil in functie zijn de elementen op verschillende vlakken
geplaatst.

Ogawa/Depardon Architects, Stadthaus an der Upper East Side, New York, 1998. Das Geländer besteht aus warm wirkendem Ahorn mit ovalem Profil und ist an einer Konstruktion aus Edelstahl befestigt. Die Belichtung des Treppenhauses erfolgt durch ein Oberlicht sowie aus den angrenzenden Räumen über lichtdurchlässige Scheiben.

Ogawa/Depardon Architects, maison de ville dans Upper East Side, New York, 1998. La rampe est en érable chaud et de forme ovale extrudée, reliée à une structure de balustrade en acier inoxydable. L'escalier est illuminé par une lucarne située en hauteur et par les panneaux translucides des pièces adjacentes.

Ogawa/Depardon Architects, Upper East Side Townhouse, New York, 1998. De leuning van warm esdoornhout is in een ovale vorm geperst en verbonden met een roestvrijstalen constructie. Door het dakraam en via de doorschijnende panelen van de aangrenzende kamers valt licht op de trap.

Gary Shoemaker Architects, Transitional Services for New York, Queens, New York, 2001. Ein ca. 1,50 m unter Geländeniveau gesetztes Gebäude steht gewissermaßen in einem „Graben", wird aber geschützt durch eine Brüstung aus Aluminium und Glas, die seiner modernen Fassade entspricht. Die Transparenz der Brüstung lässt den Komplex im überwiegend mit Wohnhäusern bebauten Queens weniger institutionell erscheinen.

Gary Shoemaker Architects, Services de transition de New York, Queens, New York, 2001. Ce bâtiment est situé 1,50 m en dessous du niveau de la rue dans une « douve », laquelle à son tour est protégée par une rampe en aluminium et en verre assortie à la façade moderniste du bâtiment. La transparence de la rampe contourne l'interdiction institutionnelle de regarder à l'intérieur de ce complexe principalement résidentiel du Queens.

Gary Shoemaker Architects, Transitional Services for New York, Queens, New York, 2001. Dit gebouw ligt 1,5 m onder straatniveau en komt uit op een 'gracht' met een leuning van geborsteld aluminium en glas die past bij de modernistische gevel. De transparante leuning voorkomt een te strenge zakelijke uitstraling van het gebouw in deze woonwijk in Queens.

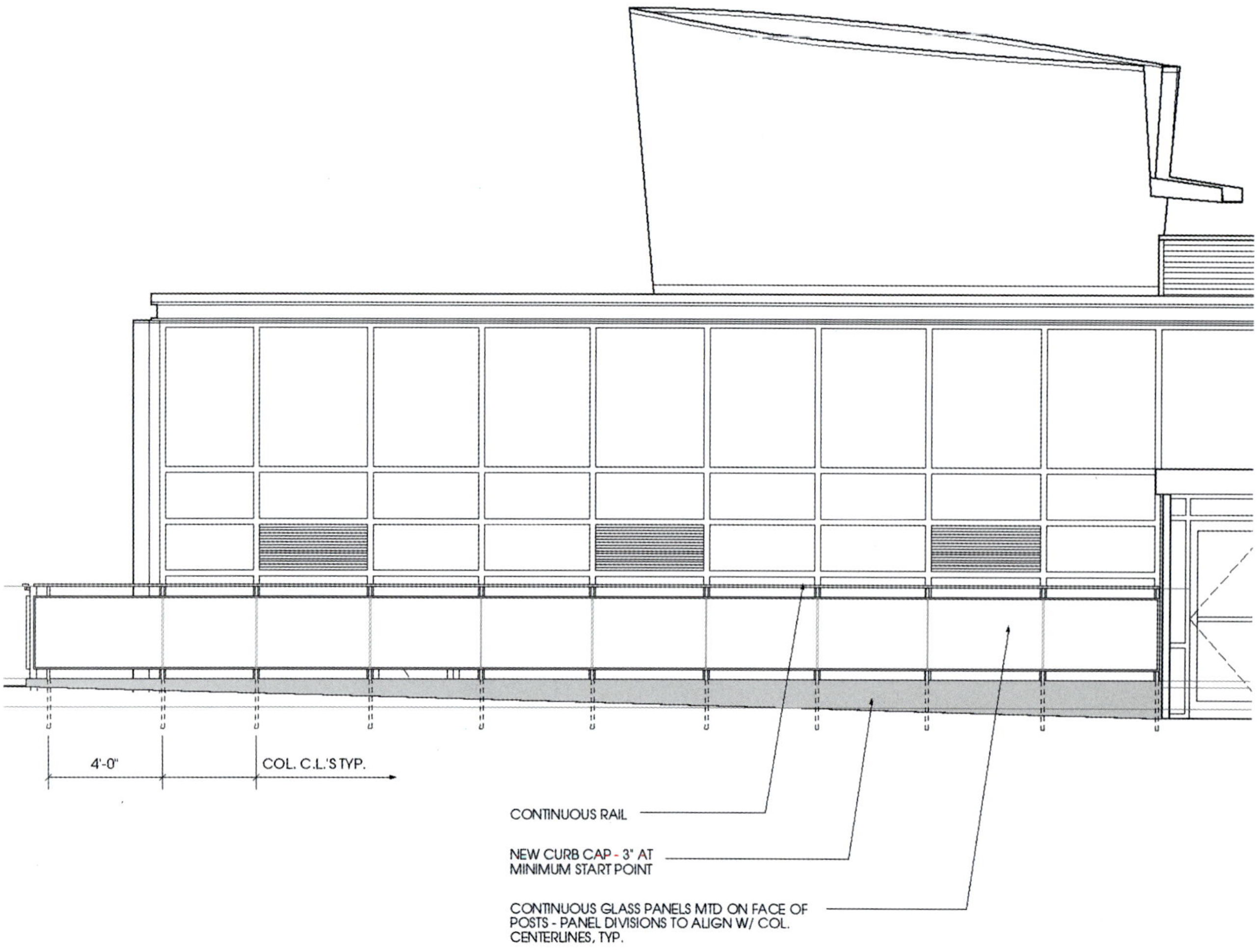

CONTINUOUS PANELS ON FACE OF POSTS

CONTINUOUS RAIL

3'-6" MINIMUM

+/- 2'-6" VIF

4"

3"

1'-0"

NEW CURB CAP - 3" AT MINIMUM START POINT

LINE OF EXIST. LIGHT WELL

4'-0"

COL. C.L.'S TYP.

CONTINUOUS RAIL

NEW CURB CAP - 3" AT MINIMUM START POINT

CONTINUOUS GLASS PANELS MTD ON FACE OF POSTS - PANEL DIVISIONS TO ALIGN W/ COL. CENTERLINES, TYP.

(1) PARTIAL ELEVATION: RAILING CONFIGURATION, TYP.
1/4"=1'-0"

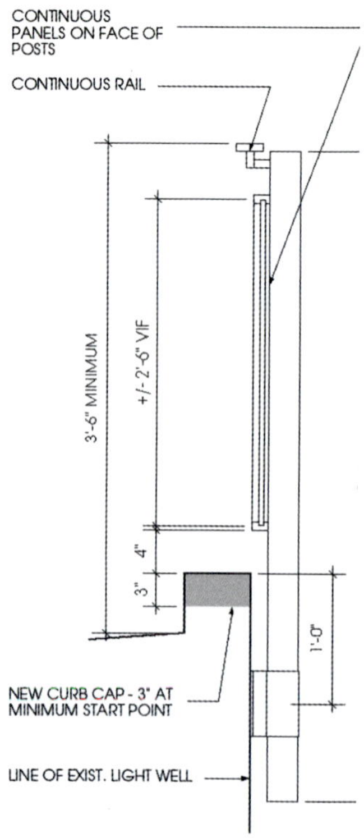

(2) DETAIL SECTION
1"=1'-0"

trennwände écrans schermen

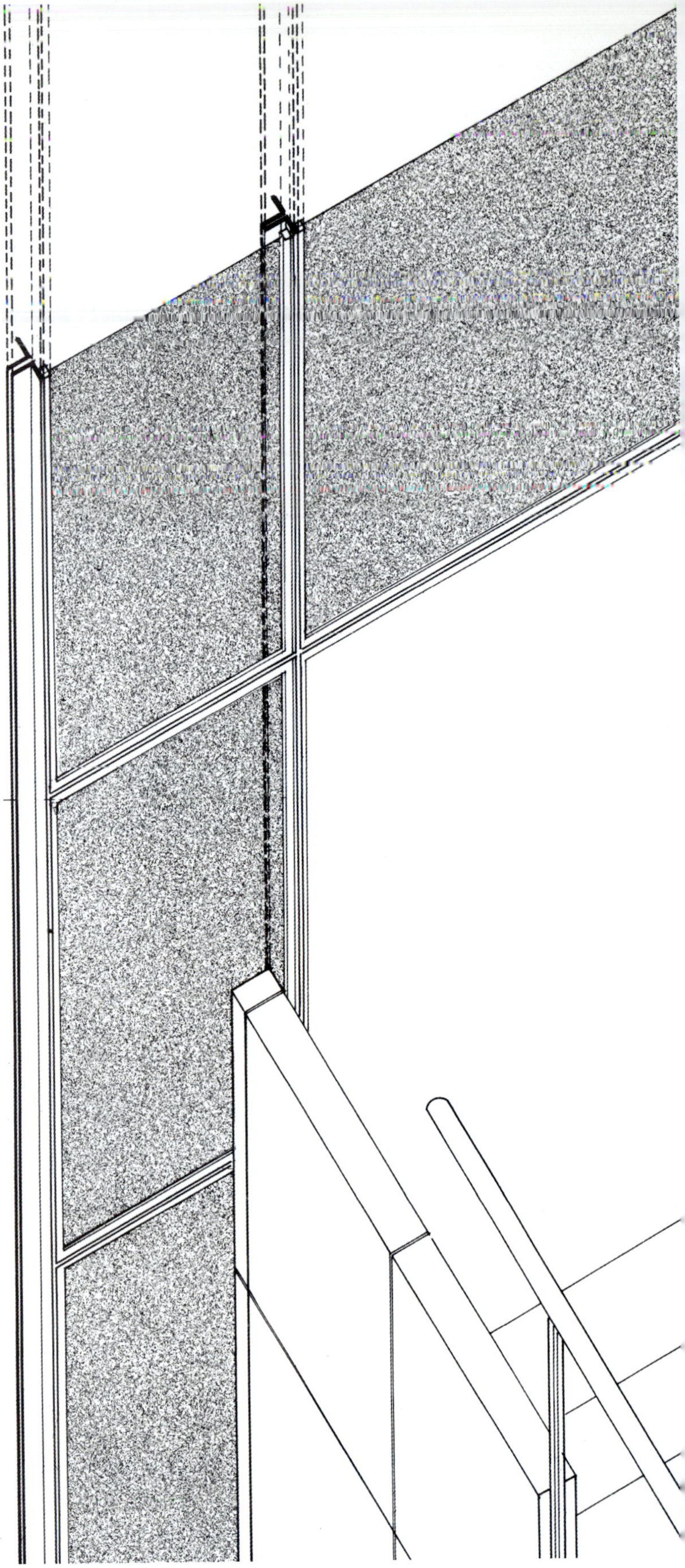

VORHERIGE SEITE: Gensler Management Consulting Offices, San Francisco, 2002. VORLIEGENDE DOPPELSEITE: Pasanella + Klein Stolzman + Berg Architects, Haus Root, Ormand Beach, Florida, 1995. Eine Trennwand aus Glas und Stahl trennt die öffentlichen von den privaten Bereichen des Hauses.

PAGE PRÉCÉDENTE : Gensler Management Consulting, San Francisco, 2002. CETTE DOUBLE PAGE : Pasanella + Klein Stolzman + Berg Architects, Root House, Ormand Beach, Floride, 1995. Un écran de verre et d'acier délimite les parties publiques et privées de la maison.

VORIGE BLADZIJDE: Gensler Management Consulting Offices, San Francisco, 2002. DEZE BLADZIJDEN: Pasanella + Klein Stolzman + Berg Architects, Root House, Ormand Beach, Florida 1995. Een scherm van glas en staal bakent de openbare en privégedeelten van het huis af.

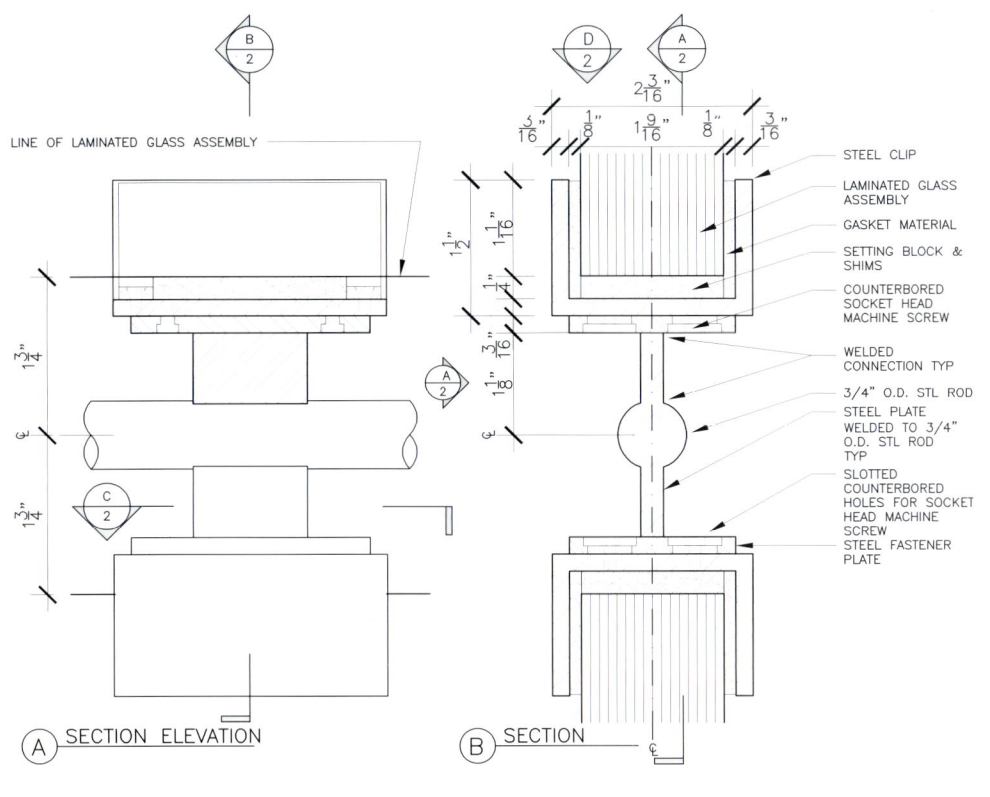

LINE OF LAMINATED GLASS ASSEMBLY

STEEL CLIP

LAMINATED GLASS ASSEMBLY

GASKET MATERIAL

SETTING BLOCK & SHIMS

COUNTERBORED SOCKET HEAD MACHINE SCREW

WELDED CONNECTION TYP

3/4" O.D. STL ROD

STEEL PLATE WELDED TO 3/4" O.D. STL ROD TYP

SLOTTED COUNTERBORED HOLES FOR SOCKET HEAD MACHINE SCREW

STEEL FASTENER PLATE

Ⓐ SECTION ELEVATION

Ⓑ SECTION

② TYPICAL HORIZONTAL/VERTICAL ROD CLIP DETAIL

François de Menil, Architekt, Byzantine Fresco Chapel Museum, Houston, 1997. Die Trennwand ist aus zahlreichen Tafeln aus Mattglas zusammengesetzt, welche die Wölbung und andere Elemente byzantinischer Architektur nachvollziehen.

François de Ménil, architecte, Musée des fresques de la chapelle byzantine, Houston, 1997. L'écran est composé de multiples panneaux soudés de verre givré qui rappellent les voûtes et d'autres éléments de l'architecture byzantine.

François de Menil, Architect, Byzantine Fresco Chapel Museum, Houston, 1997. Het scherm bestaat uit diverse matglazen panelen die het gewelf en andere elementen van de Byzantijnse architectuur doen herleven.

Krueck & Sexton Architects, Stainless Steel Apartment, Chicago, 1994. In einem von Mies van der Rohe geplanten Apartmenthaus steht eine minimalistische, durchbrochene Trennwand an einer Treppe aus Edelstahl. FOLGENDE DOPPEL-SEITE: CR Studio Architects, Ausstellungsraum Eileen Fisher, New York, 1977. Eine Trennwand aus Matt- und Klarglas wird zu einem Element à la Mondrian in der Innenausstattung, gewissermaßen zu einer abstrahierten Skulptur zur Trennung von zwei Räumen.

Krueck & Sexton Architects, appartement en acier inoxydable, Chicago, 1994. Dans un immeuble résidentiel conçu par Mies van der Rohe, un écran minimaliste de persiennes est adjacent à l'escalier d'acier inoxydable en porte-à-faux. DOUBLE PAGE SUIVANTE : CR Studio Architects, show-room Eileen Fisher, New York, 1997. Un écran de verre givré et transparent devient un élément intérieur mondrianesque, comme s'il s'agissait d'une sculpture réductrice qui sépare les deux pièces.

Krueck & Sexton Architects, Stainless Steel Apartment, Chicago, 1994. In dit door Mies van der Rohe ontworpen appartement staat een minimalistisch louverscherm naast de vrijdragende roestvrijstalen trap. VOLGENDE BLADZIJDEN: CR Studio Architects, Eileen Fisher Showroom, New York, 1997. Een scherm van mat en helder glas wordt een mondrianesk element in het interieur, alsof het een minimal-artsculptuur is die de twee kamers scheidt.

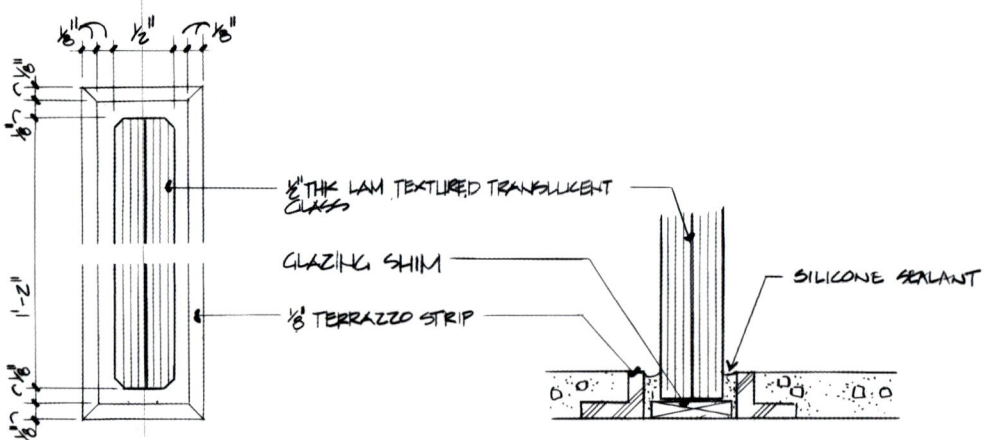

Gabellini Associates, Boutique Salvatore Ferragamo, SoHo, New York, 2001. Eine aus Panzerketten in Nickel-Silber geflochtene Metallwand verleiht den Waren in diesem Einzelhandelsgeschäft etwas Geheimnisvolles.

Gabellini Associates, boutique Salvatore Ferragamo à SoHo, New York, 2001. Un écran, formé d'un tressage chenillé en maillechort prête un soupçon de mystère au caractère mercantile de ce magasin.

Gabellini Associates, Salvatore Ferragamo Boutique SoHo, New York, 2001. Een gevlochten metalen scherm van nikkelzilveren maliën geeft de winkel iets geheimzinnigs.

TEN Arquitectos, Parkhaus, Princeton, New Jersey, 2000. Horizontale Stäbe und darin eingeflochtene vertikale Seile bilden einen Vorhang aus Edelstahl als Außenverkleidung des Parkhauses.

TEN Arquitectos, Princeton, garage, Princeton, New Jersey, 2000. Des barres horizontales et des câbles tressés verticaux forment un rideau d'acier inoxydable qui habille l'extérieur du garage.

TEN Architectos, Princeton Parking Garage, Princeton, New Jersey, 2000. De horizontale staven en verticale gevlochten kabels vormen een roestvrijstalen gordijn aan de buitenkant van de parkeergarage.

Davis Brody Bond, Valeo Thermal Systems, Hauptverwaltung für Nordamerika und Technisches Zentrum, Auburn Hills, Michigan, 1998. Ein über einer Stützenreihe in exakt berechnetem Winkel angebrachter Sonnenschutz senkt die Temperatur an der südlichen Vorhangwand.

Davis Brody Bond, Valeo Thermal Systems, siège nord-américain et centre technique, Auburn Hills, Michigan, 1998. Au-dessus d'une colonnade, des persiennes installées à un angle soigneusement calculé atténuent le gain de chaleur sur le mur-rideau orienté vers le sud.

Davis Brody Bond, Valeo Thermal Systems, North American Headquarters and Technical Center, Auburn Hills, Michigan, 1998. De onder een nauwkeurig berekende hoek geplaatste jaloezieën boven de zuilenrij weren de hitte van de gordijngevel op het zuiden.

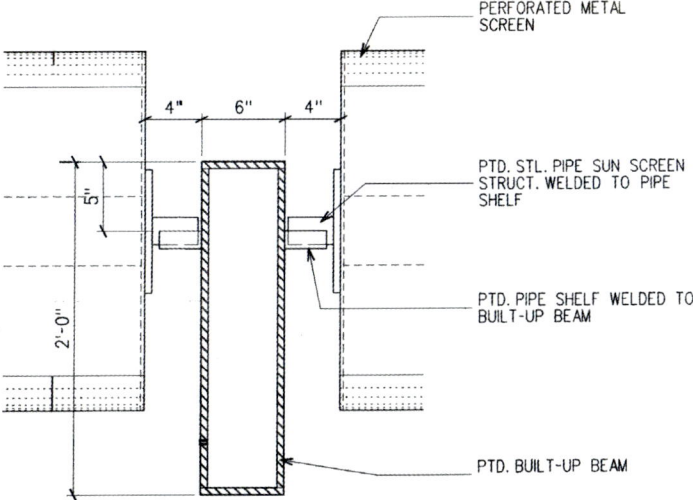

PERFORATED METAL SCREEN

PTD. STL. PIPE SUN SCREEN STRUCT. WELDED TO PIPE SHELF

PTD. PIPE SHELF WELDED TO BUILT-UP BEAM

PTD. BUILT-UP BEAM

4" 6" 4"

5"

2'-0"

B SECTION DETAIL @ SUN SCREEN
SCALE: 1½" - 1'-0"

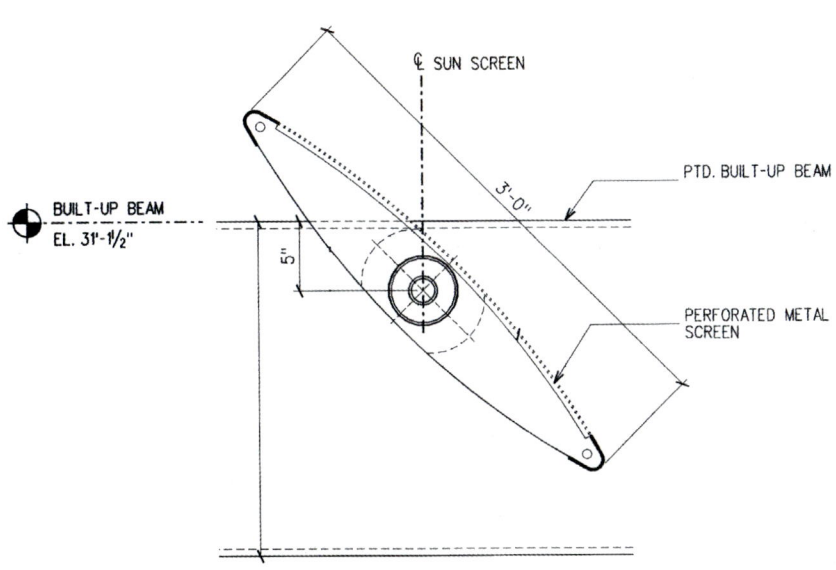

₵ SUN SCREEN

PTD. BUILT-UP BEAM

3'-0"

BUILT-UP BEAM
EL. 31'-1½"

5"

PERFORATED METAL SCREEN

A SECTION DETAIL @ SUN SCREEN
SCALE: 1½" - 1'-0"

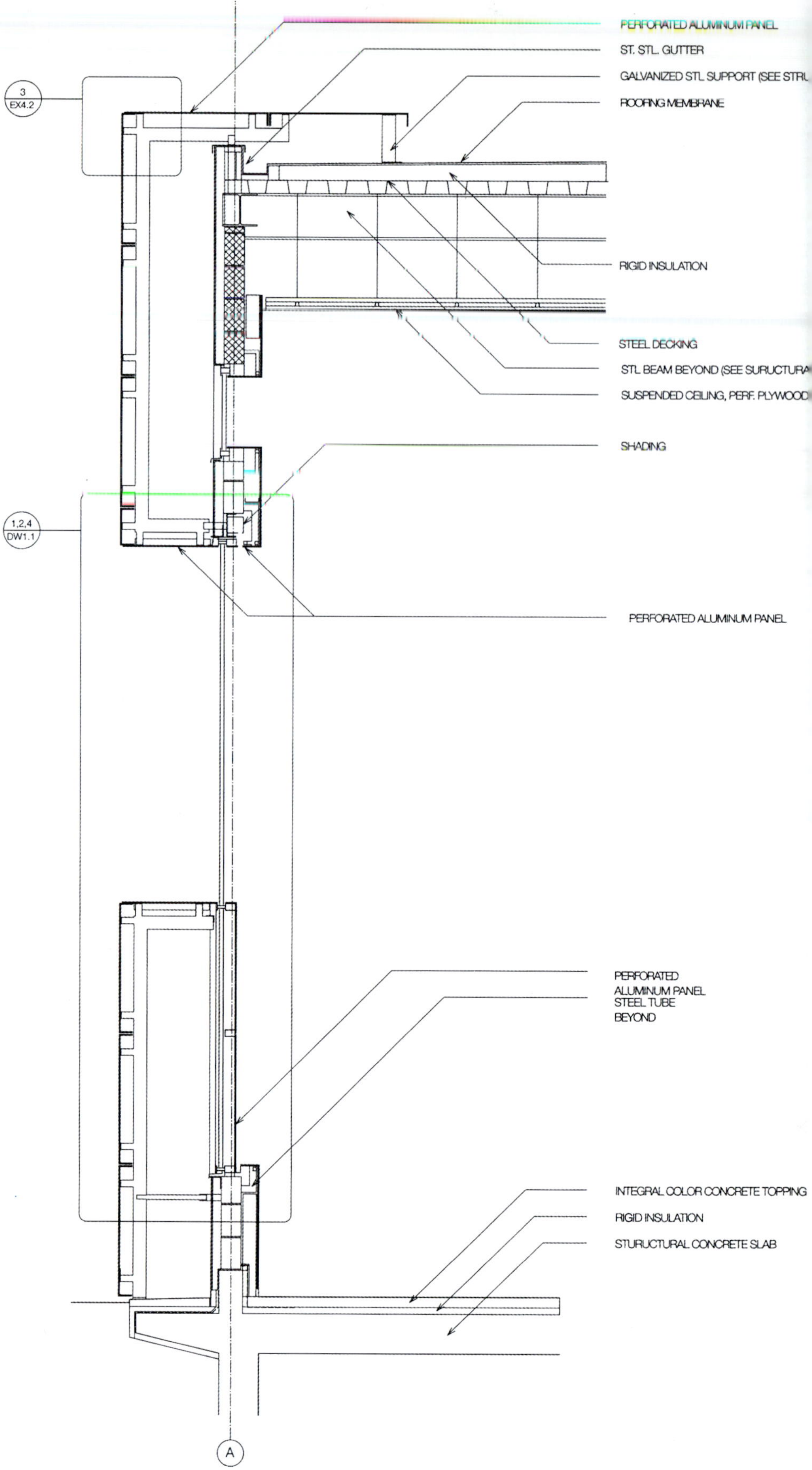

Steven Holl Architects, Bürogebäude in der Sarphatistraat, Amsterdam, 2000. Gitter an der Außenwand bilden einen starken Gegensatz zur traditionellen Backsteinarchitektur Amsterdams. Sie enthalten auch die Versorgungsleitungen sowie Belichtungs- und Belüftungselemente.

Steven Holl Architect, bureaux Sarphatistraat, Amsterdam, 2000. Des écrans extérieurs forment un contraste fortement avec l'architecture traditionnelle en brique d'Amsterdam. Ils abritent également les équipements de la maison tels que les éclairages et les grilles d'aération.

Steven Holl Architects, kantoorgebouw Sarphatistraat, Amsterdam, 2000. De gevelschermen contrasteren met de traditionele baksteenarchitectuur van Amsterdam. Ze bevatten tevens verlichting en luchtroosters.

PERFORATED ALUMINUM PANEL

ST. STL. GUTTER

GALVANIZED STL SUPPORT (SEE STRU

ROOFING MEMBRANE

RIGID INSULATION

STEEL DECKING

STL BEAM BEYOND (SEE SURUCTURA

SUSPENDED CEILING, PERF. PLYWOOD

SHADING

PERFORATED ALUMINUM PANEL

PERFORATED
ALUMINUM PANEL
STEEL TUBE
BEYOND

INTEGRAL COLOR CONCRETE TOPPING

RIGID INSULATION

STURUCTURAL CONCRETE SLAB

Steven Holl Architects, Wohnanlage Makuhari, Chiba, Japan, 1996. Hinter den perforierten Metallplatten findet sich eine große Vielfalt von Bauelementen.

Steven Holl Architects, logements Makuhari, Chiba, Japon, 1996. Les panneaux de métal perforé dissimulent une grande variété de bâtiments.

Steven Holl Architects, Makuhari Housing, Chiba, Japan, 1996. Achter de geperforeerde metalen panelen gaat een scala aan bouwelementen schuil.

einbauten placards kasten

VORHERIGE SEITE: Peter L. Gluck and Partners, Architects, Wohnhaus, Highland Park, Illinois, 1996. VORLIEGENDE DOPPELSEITE: Duccio Grassi Architects, Geschäft Max Mara, SoHo, New York, 2001. Eine kreative Verbindung von zwei Einbauelementen: Wenn Kunden in diesem Geschäft die Treppe hinaufsteigen, sehen sie eine hölzerne Ausstellungswand, an der polygonale, an der Unterseite beleuchtete Regale wie Schubladen herausragen.

PAGE PRÉCÉDENTE : Peter L. Gluck and Partners, Architects, résidence dans Highland Park, Illinois, 1998. CETTE DOUBLE PAGE : Duccio Grassi Architects, Max Mara à SoHo, New York, 2001. Une combinaison créative de deux éléments de rangement : en descendant l'escalier du magasin, les clients aperçoivent un mur d'étalage en bois, sur lequel des étagères de forme polygonale éclairées sur leur face inférieure jaillissent telles des tiroirs.

VORIGE BLADZIJDE: Peter L. Gluck & Partners, Architects, woning in Highland Park, Illinois 1998. DEZE BLADZIJDEN: Duccio Grassi Architects, Max Mara SoHo, New York, 2001. Een creatieve mix van twee kastelementen: klanten die de trap oplopen, zien een displaywand waar veelhoekige planken, met verlichting aan de onderzijde, als laden uitspringen.

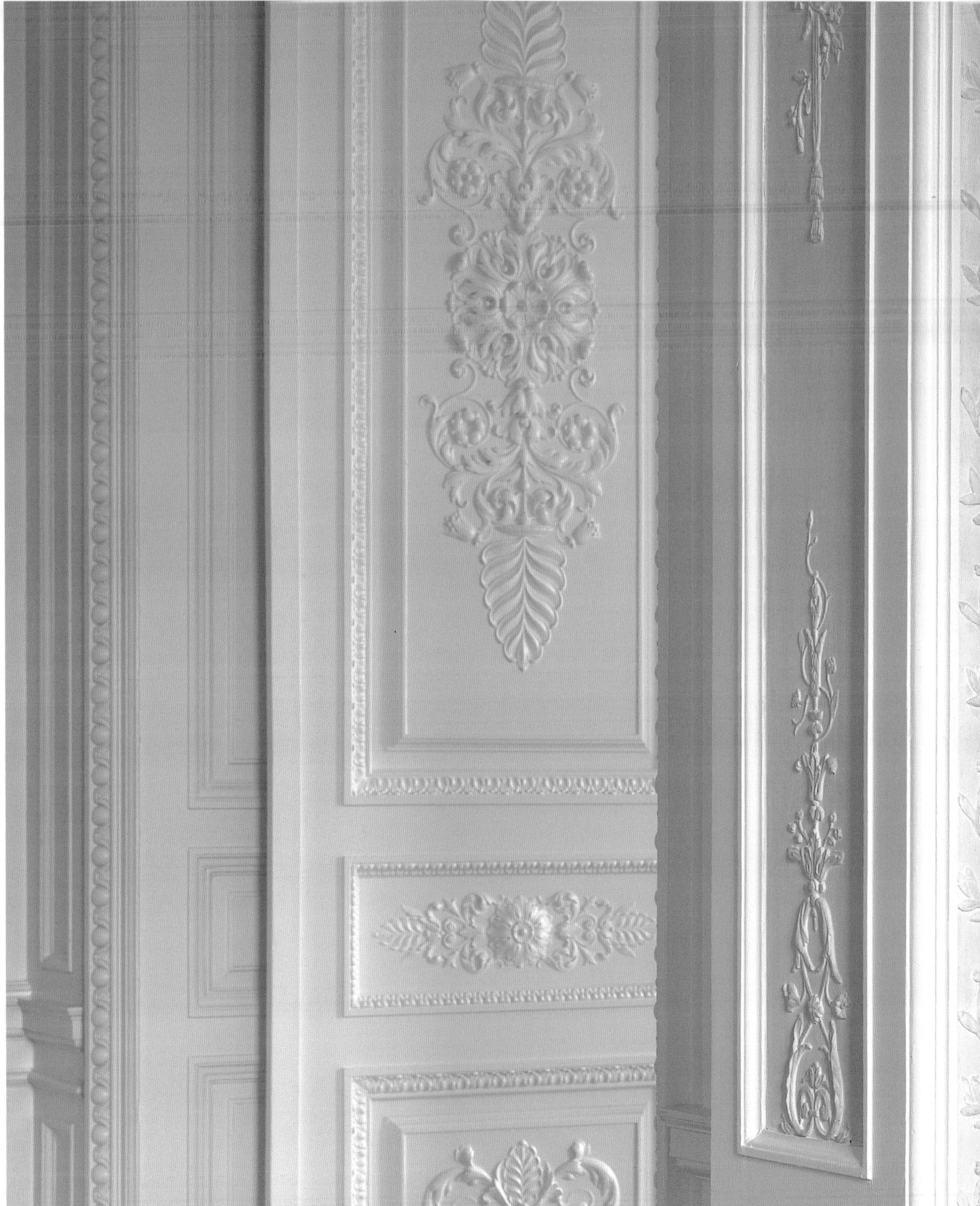

VORHERIGE DOPPELSEITE: Gabellini Associates, Ausstellungsraum Jil Sander, Hamburg, 1997. Minimalistische Gestelle aus Stahl bilden die reduzierteste Form dessen, was man sich unter einem Einbauschrank vorstellt. VORLIEGENDE DOPPELSEITE: Gabellini Associates, Boutique Jil Sander, New York, 2002. Hauchdünne Metallregale erinnern an minimalistische Skulpturen und ermöglichen eine wirkungsvolle Ausstellung der Waren.

DOUBLE PAGE PRÉCÉDENTE : Gabellini Associates, show-room Jil Sander, Hambourg, 1997. Des penderies minimalistes en acier donnent l'idée d'une armoire sous sa forme la plus réductrice. CETTE DOUBLE PAGE : Gabellini Associates, boutique Jil Sander, New York, 2002. Des étagères ultraminces en métal rappellent la sculpture minimaliste et permettent de présenter les articles de façon artistique.

VORIGE BLADZIJDEN: Gabellini Associates, Jil Sander Showroom, Hamburg, 1997. Minimalistische stalen rekken brengen het begrip kast terug tot zijn meest elementaire vorm. DEZE BLADZIJDEN: Gabellini Associates, Jil Sander Boutique, New York, 2002. Flinterdunne metalen planken, voor een kunstzinnige etalering, doen denken aan minimalistisch beeldhouwwerk.

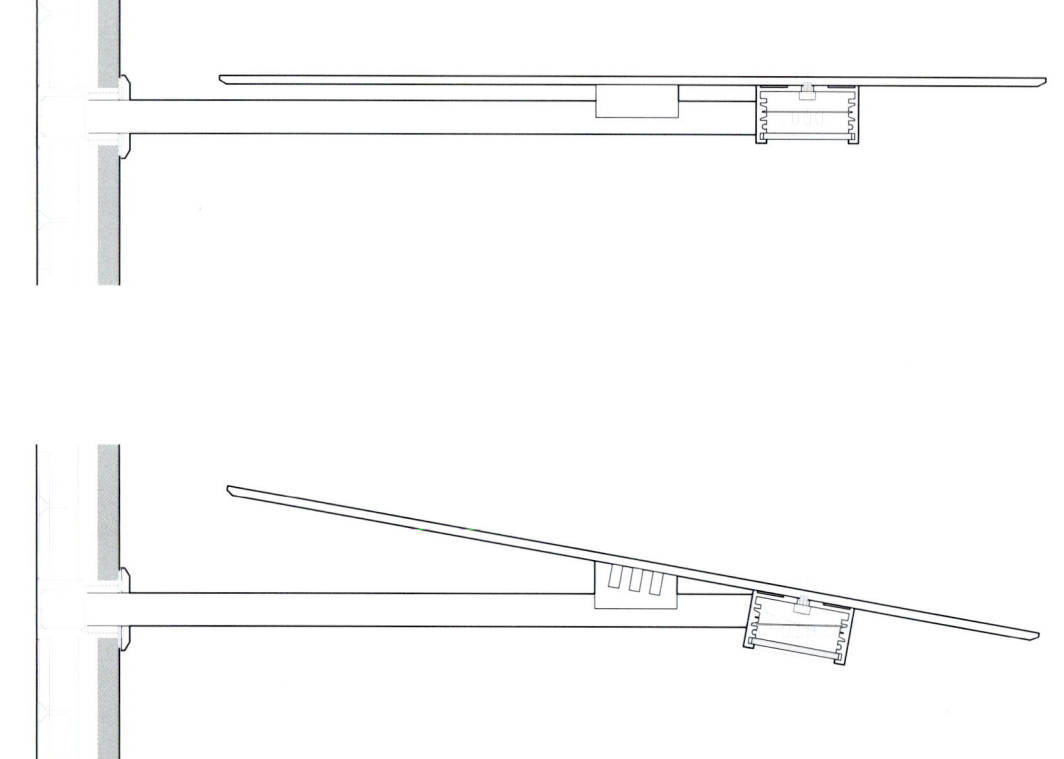

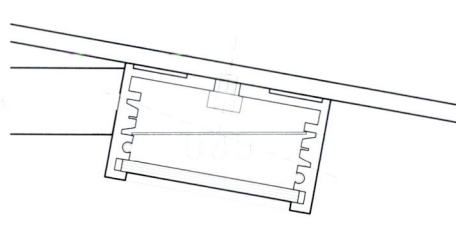

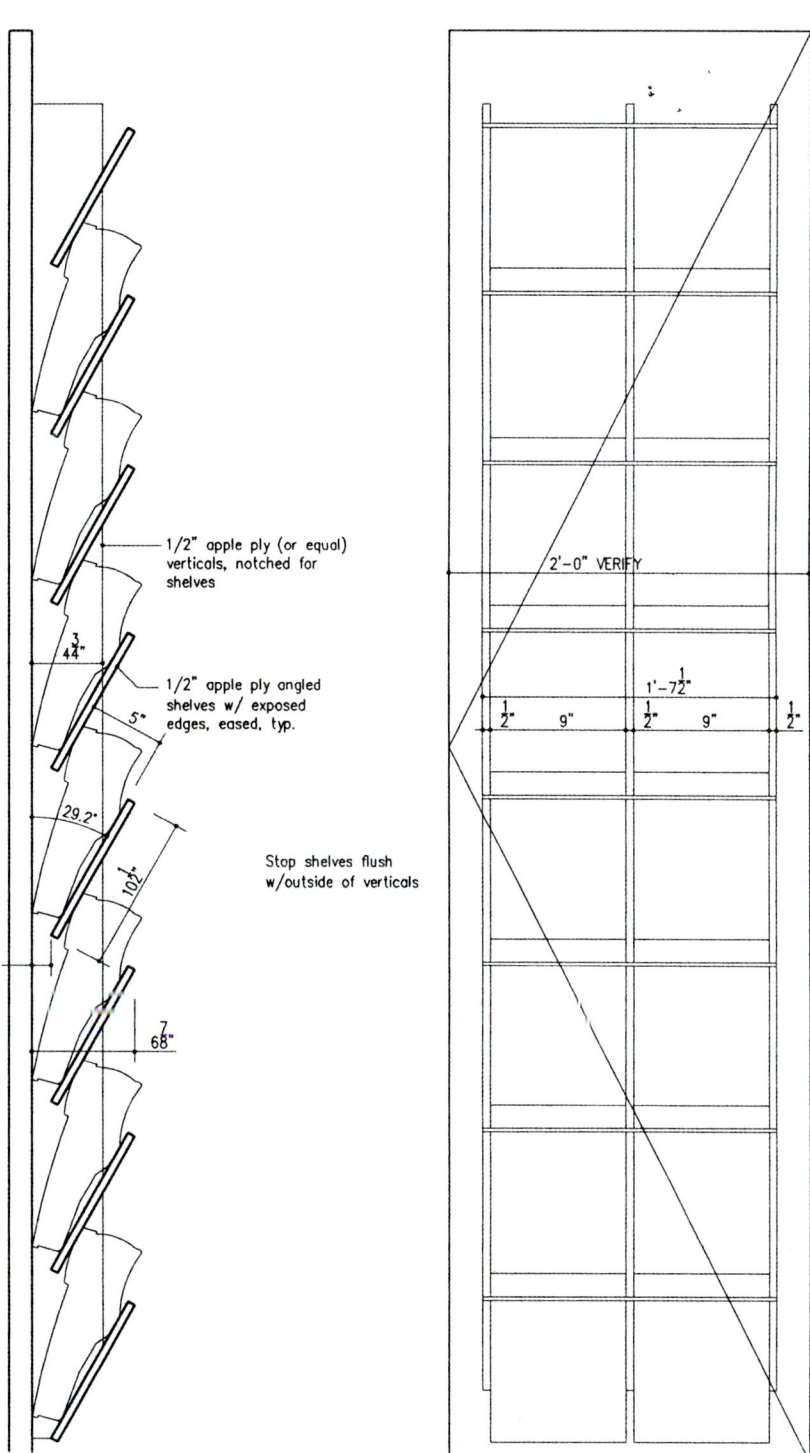

1/2" apple ply (or equal) verticals, notched for shelves

1/2" apple ply angled shelves w/ exposed edges, eased, typ.

$4\frac{3}{4}$"

5°

29.2°

$10\frac{2}{3}$"

Stop shelves flush w/outside of verticals

$6\frac{7}{8}$"

2'-0" VERIFY

1'-$7\frac{1}{2}$"

$\frac{1}{2}$" 9" $\frac{1}{2}$" 9" $\frac{1}{2}$"

Eric J. Cobb Architect, Erweiterung Haus Anderson, Seattle, 2001. Platz für alles Mögliche: Eine ganze Holzwand bildet einen elegant gestalteten Einbauschrank und enthält reichlich unterschiedlichen Stauraum.

Eric J. Cobb Architect, extension de la maison Anderson, Seattle, 2001. Cet endroit multifonctionnel, dans lequel un mur en bois entier est composé de placards élégants, offre de nombreux espaces de rangement.

Eric J. Cobb Architect, Anderson House Addition, Seattle, 2001. Voor alles is een plek; deze geheel houten wand met elegant uitgevoerde kastruimte biedt diverse opbergmogelijkheden.

Smith and Thompson Architects, Wohnung Spencer-Booker (Loft), SoHo, New York, 1997. Eine Wand, ein Schrank, ein Fenster – drei unterschiedliche Elemente sind zu einem eindrucksvollen Ergebnis verbunden.

Smith and Thompson Architects, loft Spencer-Booker, NoHo, New York, 1997. Un mur, un placard, une fenêtre : trois éléments disparates sont combinés pour obtenir un résultat spectaculaire.

Smith and Thompson Architects, Spencer-Booker Loft, NoHo, New York, 1997. Een muur, een kast, een raam: een spectaculaire combinatie van drie ongelijksoortige elementen.

Danksagung

Wir sind vielen Menschen verpflichtet, deren Hilfe für die Entstehung dieses Buches unverzichtbar war. Bei Rockport Publishers gilt unser Dank Ken Fund und Winnie Prentiss für ihre große und bedingungslose Unterstützung, das in uns gesetzte Vertrauen und die uns gewährte kreative Freiheit. Besonderer Dank gebührt Scott Cohen, Doug Dolezal, Eric Höweler, Mimi Moncier, Rob Weiner und der Chinati Foundation. Michael Decker, James McCown und Lisa Pascarelli schulden wir großen Dank für ihre Bereitschaft, sich in den kritischsten Momenten der Redaktion und Produktion an der Arbeit zu beteiligen. Rodolfo Machado und Jorge Silvetti leisteten Hilfe, ohne die dieses Projekt nie hätte realisiert werden können. Paul Warchol, der uns sein umfangreiches Archiv öffnete, können wir nicht genug danken und Respekt vor seiner Arbeit ausdrücken. Bei mehreren Besuchen in seinem Atelier und der Durchsicht Abertausender von Bildern seiner Bestände waren wir auf die freundliche Unterstützung durch Amy Barkow, Gabrielle Bendiner-Viani, Michele Convery, Bilyana Dimitrova und Ursula Warchol angewiesen. Und vor allem sind wir den kreativen Kräften verpflichtet, die allen dargestellten Details zu Grunde liegen – einer Liste von Architekten und Designern, die zu umfangreich ist, um sie hier wiedergeben zu können. Wir danken jedem von ihnen von ganzem Herzen.

Remerciements

Nous sommes redevables à de nombreuses personnes dont l'aide nous a été indispensable dans la préparation de ce livre. Chez Rockport Publishers, nous remercions en particulier Kenn Fund et Winnie Prentiss pour leur soutien franc et inconditionnel, la confiance qu'ils ont placée en nous, et la liberté créative qu'ils nous ont accordée. Nos remerciements les plus sincères vont à Scott Cohen, Doug Dolezal, Eric Höweler, Mimi Moncier et Rob Weiner ainsi qu'à la Fondation Chinati. À Michael Decker, James McCown et Lisa Pasacarelli, nous sommes particulièrement reconnaissants de leur disponibilité aux moments les plus délicats de l'édition et de la production. Rodolfo Machado et Jorge Silvetti ont apporté un soutien sans lequel cet ouvrage n'aurait jamais vu le jour. À Paul Warchol, qui a ouvert ses vastes archives photographiques, nous ne pourrons jamais assez témoigner de notre reconnaissance ni de notre respect pour son œuvre. Au cours de plusieurs visites à son studio et pendant que nous nous plongions parmi ses milliers et milliers d'images, nous dépendions de l'aimable assistance d'Amy Barkow, Gabrielle Bendiner-Viani, Michele Convery, Bilyana Dimitrova et Ursula Warchol. Et par-dessus tout, nous restons redevables envers les créateurs de ces détails que nous présentons, c'est-à-dire à des architectes et designers si nombreux que nous ne pouvons tous les citer. Chacun mérite nos remerciements les plus chaleureux.

Dankbetuiging

We zijn velen dank verschuldigd voor hun onmisbare hulp bij de totstandkoming van dit boek. We bedanken Ken Fund en Winnie Prentiss van Rockport Publishers voor hun grote en onvoorwaardelijke steun, het vertrouwen dat ze in ons stelden en de creatieve speelruimte die ze ons boden. Een bijzonder woord van dank gaat uit naar Scott Cohen, Doug Dolezal, Eric Höweler, Mimi Moncier, Rob Weiner en de Chinati Foundation. Dank ook aan Michael Decker, James McCown en Lisa Pascarelli voor hun bereidwillige hulp op de moeilijkste momenten van redactie en productie. Zonder de steun van Rodolfo Machado en Jorge Silvetti was dit project er nooit gekomen. We spreken, met groot respect voor zijn werk, onze dank uit aan Paul Warchol voor het openstellen van zijn uitgebreide fotoverzameling. Tijdens de verschillende bezoeken aan zijn atelier, toen we de vele duizenden afbeeldingen in zijn archief doorzochten, konden ons verlaten op de steun van Amy Barkow, Gabrielle Bendiner-Viani, Michele Convery, Bilyana Dimitrova en Ursula Warchol. Onze allergrootste en welgemeende dank gaat uit naar de creatieve krachten, de architecten en ontwerpers – te veel om hier op te noemen – achter de details in dit boek.